Gill Paul is an author of historical fiction and non-fiction, whose books include the popular *World War I Love Stories* and *World War II Love Stories* (both 2014). Among her other published works are the novels *Women and Children First* (2012) and *The Affair* (2013).

Camilla Tominey is Royal Editor of the *Sunday Express*. She is also a royal contributor to *Good Morning Britain* and a royal expert on the US television network NBC.

INSTRUMENT OF ABDICATION

I, Edward the Eighth, of Great
Britain, Ireland, and the British Dominions
beyond the Seas, King, Emperor of India, do
hereby declare My irrevocable determination
to renounce the Throne for Myself and for
My descendants, and My desire that effect
should be given to this Instrument of
Abdication immediately.

In token whereof I have hereunto set
My hand this tenth day of December, nineteen
hundred and thirty six, in the presence of
the witnesses whose signatures are subscribed.

SIGNED AT
FORT BELVEDERE
IN THE PRESENCE
OF

Edward RI

Albert

Henry

George

LOLA MONTES.
COUNTESS OF LANDSFELD.

ROYAL

LOVE STORIES

The tales behind the real-life romances of Europe's kings & queens

GILL PAUL

Introduction by Camilla Tominey

Ivy Press

For my lovely friend Katie, who used to be Princess of Calvi

First published in the UK in 2015 by
Ivy Press
210 High Street
Lewes
East Sussex BN7 2NS
United Kingdom
www.ivypress.co.uk

British Library Cataloging-in-Publication Data

A catalogue record for this book is available from the British Library

ISBN: 978-1-78240-150-6

This book was conceived, designed and produced by

Ivy Press

Creative Director Peter Bridgewater

Publisher Susan Kelly

Art Director Wayne Blades

Senior Editor Jayne Ansell

Designer Andrew Milne

Picture Researcher Katie Greenwood

Printed in China

Colour origination by Ivy Press Reprographics

Distributed worldwide (except North America) by
Thames & Hudson Ltd., 181A High Holborn, London WC1V 7QX
United Kingdom

10 9 8 7 6 5 4 3 2 1

CONTENTS

Introduction—*6*

Peter I of Portugal & Inês de Castro—*20*

Inês was his wife's lady-in-waiting but Peter couldn't help loving her with an all-consuming passion that drove him mad after her death

Shah Jahan & Mumtaz Mahal—*32*

Shah Jahan couldn't bear to be separated from Mumtaz for a single day, and he designed a mausoleum that would preserve the memory of their love for eternity

Catherine the Great & Grigory Potemkin—*44*

Catherine had many royal favorites but Grigory was the only one who kept his place in the royal heart after the flames of lust had cooled

Louis XVI & Marie Antoinette—*56*

They were naive teenagers when they married and Louis and Marie Antoinette didn't have much in common, but they came to care genuinely for each other

Napoleon Bonaparte & Joséphine de Beauharnais—*68*

The famous military general Napoleon fell passionately in love with his gentle, sensuous Joséphine—but there was one thing she couldn't give him

Ludwig I of Bavaria & Lola Montez—*80*

Lola was a badly behaved showgirl with a talent for seduction, and Ludwig paid the ultimate price for his obsession with her

Victor Emmanuel II & Rosa Vercellana—*92*

The prince and the peasant girl: it sounds like a fairy tale but for Victor and Rosa it was true love, even if she would never become queen

Rudolph, Crown Prince of Austria, & Baroness Mary Vetsera—*104*

While waiting in line for the throne, Rudolph attracted a naive young admirer named Mary Vetsera, who would do whatever he asked of her

Nicholas II & Alexandra—*116*

They fell in love as children and fought to be allowed to marry, but revolution was in the air and their days on the imperial throne were numbered

Edward VIII & Wallis Simpson—*128*

Ambitious Wallis finally got her king but not in the way she had wanted, and the repercussions of their romance made headlines around the globe

Prince Bertil of Sweden & Lilian Craig—*140*

Prevented from marrying by Sweden's laws of succession, they still chose to be together, even though it involved great sacrifice along the way

Prince Rainier III & Grace Kelly—*152*

Hollywood royalty marries into European monarchy: it was a match created by a French magazine, a priest, and a host of lawyers before Grace and Rainier knew much about each other

King Hussein of Jordan & Lisa Halaby—*164*

From a privileged upbringing in America to queen of an Arabic state is a big leap, but King Hussein proposed marriage to Lisa only two weeks after their first date

Prince William & Catherine Middleton—*176*

William and Kate started dating in college but he was wary of commitment after what had happened to his mother, the late Princess Diana

Introduction

by Camilla Tominey

AN ENDURING LOVE

*T*he public's fascination with royalty dates as far back as the days of ancient Egypt. With their untold riches and powerful positions at the top of the social hierarchy, for centuries Pharaohs and Emperors, Kings and Queens have enthralled and appalled in equal measure. Yet the allure of monarchy has continued beyond the superficial sparkle of the crown jewels.

ABOVE
Dubbed the "Great Royal Wife," Queen Nefertiti is depicted here alongside Egyptian Pharaoh Akhenaten and their children, worshipping their one God, Aten.

Behind the razzle-dazzle of royal life, it is the relationships at the heart of history's most illustrious dynasties that have proved so compelling. Of all the tales to have come out of court over the years, it is the royal love stories that have endured the most.

In a world where every little girl dreams of being a princess and every little boy dreams of being a king, it is little wonder royal love stories have captivated audiences since time immemorial. Immortalized in the history books and retold on stage and screen, they are the fantasies that have become reality—fiction that has become fact before our very eyes. Over the course of history we have watched as affairs of the heart have unfolded into affairs of state. We have witnessed ordinary lives made extraordinary by royal betrothal, celebrated marital successes, and shared spousal sorrows. We have seen royal mistresses revered and reviled—their Kings abhorred and adored.

Unlike most fairy tales, not all royal love stories have a happy ending. For royals, having to rule with their heads and not their hearts has made relationships far from straightforward. With great power comes great responsibility, and when royals have had to choose between love and the crown, the consequences have at times been constitutionally catastrophic, resulting in abdication and even death. Other royals have been luckier in love, somehow managing to balance their personal and public lives to benefit not only themselves but also their subjects.

Indeed, history suggests that it is the monarchs in the most stable, loving relationships who have proved the most popular, while those with tumultuous love lives have found themselves mistrusted by the public as much as in private.

From the days of the ancient dynasties until the thoroughly modern monarchies of the 21st century, the obstacles to royal relationships have remained as unchanged as our fascination with those who have royally loved and often lost.

LOVE YOUR COUNTRY

The notion of marriage being based entirely on love is a relatively new concept when it comes to royal weddings, which have been "arranged" since the days of the Norman Conquest in 1066. In fact, it is only relatively recently, in the last century or so, that sovereigns have been allowed to choose their own spouses.

Historically, it has not always been a case of marrying royalty to royalty to keep the bloodlines as blue as possible, although one need only look at the royal families of Europe to see the consequences of marrying within such a limited gene pool—the hereditary blood-clotting disease hemophilia being so widespread during the 19th and 20th centuries that it was popularly referred to as "the Royal Disease." The match-making of one monarchy with another had as much to do with politics as interbreeding. Kings married to forge unions with fellow dynasties in a bid to expand their empires, both figuratively and geographically.

Such dynastic marriages can be traced back to the Pharaohs, when they were a common means of establishing political allegiances and trade partnerships, and were even used to broker peace. In Roman times, daughters were used as a form of currency to strengthen the military position of the family. This practice continued well into the 19th century when European princesses were promised as babies to the sons of neighboring countries as a form of empire-building.

In many cases, the marriages would happen when the princesses were still very young girls. They would remain with their families until it was deemed the right time for them to be shipped off to their husbands. Marie Antoinette, the daughter of Maria Theresa, Queen of Hungary and Bohemia, was one such princess, having been promised to the Crown Prince of France, later King Louis XVI, when she was just twelve years old.

As such it was not uncommon for royal couples never to have met before saying "I do." Even in more modern royal marriages, such as that of Prince Rainier and Grace Kelly, the couple had only met a handful of times before becoming engaged. Rainier III, like many rulers before him, was coming under increasing pressure to find a wife who would produce the heir needed to guarantee the future of his royal line. Had he produced no legitimate children, Monaco would have reverted back to France under the terms of the Franco-Monegasque treaty signed in 1918.

He was not the first king to be pressured into marriage, albeit a happy one, to produce an heir, and he won't be the last. Indeed, history threatened to repeat itself when his only son, Prince Albert, failed to produce any legitimate children. But fortunately for them, new laws similar to those to be introduced across the Commonwealth protect modern monarchs if they do not have any of their own children, by passing the throne to one of their siblings, even if the sibling is female.

EARLY MARRIAGE CONTRACTS

Ancient marriage contracts dating back to Egyptian times set out property rights and contain little reference to the act of marriage itself. The phrase *shep en shemet* is frequently used, meaning the "price" for marrying a woman. Traditionally, the contract would not even be between the bride and groom, but the groom and the bride's father, and this continued to be the unspoken rule up until as recently as the last century. Dowries would commonly be drawn up when royals became engaged, specifying how much should be paid by the bride's family upon marriage. Since medieval times, marriages appear to have been made up of two stages: the betrothal and the subsequent wedding. The betrothal was treated as the act of bestowing a woman on a man while the wedding served as a celebration of him taking possession of her.

LEFT
Arguably one of history's most controversial queens, Marie Antoinette's marriage to Louis XVI led to her downfall. Accused of promiscuity and profligacy, she contributed to the abolition of the French monarchy and was executed in October 1793.

MISTRESSES

Forced into empty, loveless marriages with princesses they barely knew, and in some cases had never met, it is hardly surprising that kings have historically taken mistresses. While England's Henry VIII will arguably go down in history as the monarch who struggled with monogamy more than any other, infidelity has been so rife since medieval times that the taking of a mistress has long been regarded as a royal rite of passage. Indeed, in the 16th, 17th, and 18th centuries, European kings were frowned upon if they did not embark on an extramarital affair. And even when royal love matches proved successful, leading to loving and lasting relationships, it was still commonplace for a king to take a mistress alongside his wife.

The courting of courtesans was not just for carnal pleasure. Kings did not only turn to their lovers for sex, but also for advice and conversation, resulting in mistresses sometimes wielding a great deal of power behind the throne. In the 1540s and '50s, the French King Henri II's mistress, Diane de Poitiers, imposed taxes, appointed ministers, and passed laws. As well as providing a listening ear,

BELOW
Cartoonist William Hogarth's 18th-century satirical print sums up the mood as Cardinal Wolsey cringes at the sight of King Henry VIII leading Anne Boleyn, the second of his six wives, to Court after divorcing Catherine of Aragon in 1533.

mistresses were expected to deploy their charm as a weapon against foreign ambassadors and to promote the arts. They would attend religious services daily, give alms to the poor, and turn their jewels in to the treasury at times of war. In return, mistresses were given official titles, generous allowances, and even pensions. The most successful mistresses accumulated great personal wealth, which made for intense competition among ladies seeking to catch the eye of the king.

As a result, while mistresses were pampered and afforded great privileges, they also lived a life in limbo, not knowing from one day to the next whether they were about to be replaced. While some could look forward to "retiring" rich and living happily ever after once they had served their purpose, others were not so lucky. Falling out of favor cost some of them their lives, as two of Henry VIII's concubines, Anne Boleyn and Catherine Howard, discovered after marrying the King. The hedonistic lifestyles of other mistresses, such as Lola Montez, earned a level of public disapproval that ultimately led to their downfall. After the upheavals of the French Revolution, a more conservative politics and a new moral climate grew up across Europe—a shift toward monogamous family units and traditional values. However, this did not stop kings from taking mistresses, though rather than being worn as badges of honor, extramarital affairs were now kept strictly under wraps.

Sometimes kings went on to father many illegitimate children from taking so many mistresses. Henry I of England had so many bastard children—perhaps as many as twenty-five—that the historian Chris Given-Wilson has commented, "It might be permissible to wonder how he managed to keep track of them all." Charles II fathered at least twenty illegitimate children, of which he acknowledged fourteen. Henry VIII tried to change the rule which banned illegitimate children from claiming any succession rights with the birth of his bastard son, Henry FitzRoy. FitzRoy (*roi* being French for "king") was a surname commonly given to illegitimate children of monarchs as a nod to birthrights they would never be allowed to claim. In any case, Henry FitzRoy died of consumption before Henry VIII's wishes could be realized.

ABOVE
Alice Frederica Keppel, a long-term mistress of King Edward VII, is the great-grandmother of Camilla Parker-Bowles, who married Prince Charles in 2005 following a lengthy affair.

THE RICH & THE POOR

Historically, and somewhat strangely, the masses have been far more accepting of monarchs marrying one of their own rather than one of "us." Part of the problem was that by marrying someone of lesser status, a king was perceived to have diluted the royal bloodline. As a result, monarchs who refused to forsake their socially inferior spouses were forced into morganatic marriages, preventing their succession rights or other titles and privileges from being passed onto their wives or any children born of the marriage. Such marriages were also known as "left-handed," because in the wedding ceremony the groom traditionally held his bride's right hand with his left hand instead of his right. Occasionally, children of morganatic marriages have ended up succeeding to their family's realms. Margrave Leopold inherited the throne of Baden, despite being born of a morganatic marriage, after all the dynastic males of the House of Zähringen died out. His descendants ruled the grand duchy until the abolition of the monarch in 1918. Although ineligible to succeed their family's respective thrones, children of morganatic marriages often achieved dynastic success elsewhere by marrying into other European royal families. Mary of Teck, the daughter from the morganatic marriage of Duke Alexander of Württemberg and Claudine Rhédey von Kis-Rhéde, went on to become Queen in 1911 after marrying King George V.

The concept of morganatic marriage has always been a rather European construct and has never properly existed in England, where historically the crown has descended through marriages with commoners. King Edward III's son John of Gaunt married commoner Katherine Swynford after they had been cohabiting for several years. All their children born previously were legitimated by an Act of Parliament.

In 1923, the future King George VI, the present Queen's father, became the first future English monarch to marry a non-princess since 1660 when the future James II eloped with Anne Hyde. In that earlier case, although nearly everyone, including the bride's father, urged them not to marry, they tied the knot in secret by going

BELOW
Commoner Anne Hyde's marriage to James, Duke of York, later King James II and VII, caused much gossip, not least because she gave birth to the couple's child just two months after they married in 1660.

through an official marriage ceremony in London. Anne was a devoted wife and influenced many of James's decisions as "heir presumptive," but died in 1671.

While in the last century or so the public has generally been more sympathetic when kings have fallen for so-called commoners, constitutionally it has proven no less disastrous. In Edward VIII's case, falling for a commoner who also happened to be an American and a divorcee cost him the crown. The 1936 abdication crisis remains the most cited modern example of the constitutional catastrophe threatened by monarchs who fall in love with the "wrong" person.

Conversely, when it appeared likely that Prince Bertil of Sweden would become regent, he decided not to marry Welsh commoner Lilian Craig because it would cost him the crown. The couple lived together discreetly for decades until the young King Carl XVI Gustaf had himself married and secured the succession of the Swedish crown, whereupon the marriage of Bertil and Lilian could finally take place, decades after their first meeting.

ABOVE
Elizabeth Bowes-Lyon twice turned down the Duke of York's marriage proposal, fearing she would "never again be free to think, speak, and act as I feel I really ought to." Eventually in January 1923 she agreed to marry "Bertie," despite her misgivings about royal life.

MODERN ROYALS

These days European royals tend to marry for love and not out of a desire to build empires, largely because modern royal families have far less political influence than previous generations. The tradition of royalty marrying royalty has been turned on its head, and in the 21st century it is unusual for royals not to marry commoners. Indeed, those who decide against marrying "beneath" them risk being perceived as aloof and out of touch.

Of course there is still a pervasive sense of "them" and "us" when it comes to royalty, but today's royal marriage ceremony is the same as any other—the only difference being the status of the celebrant and the size of the congregation, not to mention the millions watching the televised proceedings at home. Such is the public's fascination with royal love stories that every aspect of their weddings is now scrutinized in the name of entertainment. When royal brides-to-be are as photogenic as Grace Kelly, Diana Spencer, and Kate Middleton, then speculation about the wedding dress can reach fever pitch. They walk down the aisle as mere women and emerge as style icons. Perceived as the archetypal fairy tale royal wedding at the time, Charles and Diana's 1981 nuptials had an estimated global audience of 750

ABOVE
South African swimming champion Charlene Wittstock married Prince Albert II of Monaco in a spectacular two-day ceremony in July 2011 wearing a custom-made Armani wedding gown.

RESTRICTIONS ON LOVE

The Royal Marriages Act 1772 has, until very recently, given the British sovereign the right of veto over any royal marriage deemed to diminish the throne. It was drafted in 1771 by King George III, as a direct consequence of his brother Prince Henry marrying the commoner Anne Horton. At the time, he was not aware that another brother, Prince William Henry, had secretly married Maria, the illegitimate daughter of the British politician Sir Edward Walpole, five years earlier. The King was said to have been furious that both brothers had entered into such unsuitable alliances when he had been forced to marry for what he called purely dynastic reasons. By declaring that any royal marriages carried out without the consent of the monarch would be null and void, the Act proved highly controversial when it received Royal Assent on April 1, 1772. In 2013, the Succession to the Crown Act 2013 was drafted, proposing the Act be limited to the first six people in line to the throne. If it comes into effect after also being implemented by the other Commonwealth realms, the new Act will repeal the Royal Marriages Act 1772 in its entirety.

LEFT
Charles and Diana were not even able to escape the press on their honeymoon, pictured here on the Queen's Balmoral estate in the Scottish Highlands, following their wedding on July 29, 1981.

MODERN SUCCESSION

Only recently, new laws abolishing male primogeniture have brought monumental constitutional change to monarchies across Europe. In April 2002, Monaco promulgated Princely Law 1.249, which provides that if a reigning prince dies without surviving legitimate issue, the throne passes to his legitimate siblings and their legitimate descendants of both sexes. And in 2009, Denmark amended the Act of Succession of 1953, which allowed a woman to inherit the throne only if she had no older or younger brothers. The amendment meant that primogeniture no longer put males above females and thus allowed the eldest-born child of a monarch to inherit the throne regardless of gender. In Britain, the Succession to the Crown Act 2013 removes the centuries-old rule of male primogeniture. Before the Act, daughters born to monarchs would be superseded in succession to the crown by a younger brother, but once the new Act has been fully brought into force across the Commonwealth, males born after October 28, 2011, will no longer overtake their elder sisters in the royal line.

million, making it the most popular program ever broadcast. The *New York Times* estimated that 3 billion people watched William and Kate tie the knot in 2011. The trials and tribulations of modern royal marriages are played out in the media for everyone to follow. While the British Royal Family continues to generate the most headlines around the world, European newspapers and magazines remain full of gossip concerning their Continental cousins, with Monaco's Grimaldi dynasty seemingly as enthralling as it was in Grace Kelly's day.

There is still an onus on royal newlyweds to produce heirs, as was witnessed when Prince William married Kate Middleton. It was not long after the royal bride had walked down the aisle that the public, both in Britain and across the world, started speculating about when we would hear the pitter-patter of tiny royal feet.

Prince George's birth on July 22, 2013, at St. Mary's in London may have echoed Prince William's because he was born at the same hospital, but really it heralded the start of a brand-new era for the House of Windsor and showed how the monarchy has modernized. In contrast to Diana's shy, silent appearance on the steps of the Lindo Wing in 1982, Kate shared equal billing with her husband. Each took turns speaking to the press and holding the newborn, leaving royal watchers with the down-to-earth image of William fitting the baby seat into the back of the car and driving his new family home.

While in the olden days kings and queens were expected to rule with their heads and not their hearts, today they are expected to rule with both, just as future monarchs like Prince William, Frederick, Crown Prince of Denmark, and Crown Princess Victoria of Sweden are all under pressure to get the balance right between their public and private lives.

It has taken only four centuries, but it seems that monarchy has finally managed to catch up with the times.

ABOVE
The dawning of a new royal era on the steps of the Lindo Wing, St. Mary's Hospital, London, following the birth of Prince George Alexander Louis of Cambridge on July 22, 2013.

OPPOSITE
Modern European royals Crown Prince Frederick of Denmark and Victoria, Crown Princess of Sweden, accompany each other to a gala reception at Christisansborg Palace in the Danish capital Copenhagen in May 2007.

Peter I of Portugal
– & –
Inês de Castro

Pedro (Peter)
Born: April 8, 1320, Coimbra, Portugal
Died: January 18, 1367, Estremoz, Portugal

Inês Pérez de Castro y Valadares
Sánchez de Castilla
Born: 1325, Galicia
Died: January 7, 1355, Coimbra, Portugal

Married: possibly in 1354

Peter watched from shore as the ship bringing his bride,
Constance of Peñafiel, arrived in Lisbon harbor. He spotted a beautiful
blonde-haired girl with a "heron neck" and thought she must be his wife,
then was very disappointed to learn that she was one of Constance's
ladies-in-waiting—a girl by the name of Inês de Castro.

*D*uring the Middle Ages, marriages in the Portuguese royal
family were part of a complex game of diplomacy with their
neighbors in the various kingdoms of Spain, of which the
most powerful was Castile. Matches were frequently arranged as soon
as a child had survived its earliest years. In 1322, Peter's eldest sister,
Maria, was married to King Alfonso XI of Castile and in exchange
in 1325 Peter was married to Blanche of Castile, Alfonso's cousin.
He was just five years old and Blanche was ten when the wedding
took place, but eight years later the marriage was annulled on grounds
that it had not been consummated and no heir had resulted.

Alfonso XI had a mistress and refused to give her up after the
marriage, so in 1335 Maria fled back to the Portuguese court. Peter's
father was incensed by this ill treatment of his daughter, so in an act of
retaliation he decided to marry the sixteen-year-old Peter to Alfonso's
ex-wife, Constance of Peñafiel, who also happened to be the daughter
of a political opponent of Alfonso. Constance still lived in Castile,
so a proxy bride stood in for her during the ceremony in Portugal.
When he heard the news, King Alfonso was so enraged he held
Constance hostage and wouldn't let her travel to Portugal, but it made
no difference, as legally the pair were married. The Portuguese King
Afonso IV and the Castilian King Alfonso XI continued their quarrel
for four years, until they were forced to unite against a common
enemy, the Sultan of Morocco. At that stage Constance was freed
to come to Lisbon and finally meet Peter, the young man to whom
she'd long been married.

While the staff at the castle prepared a huge banquet, the people
of Lisbon, including Peter, descended on the dock to watch the
arrival of Constance's fleet. It was full of Castilian nobles and ladies
accompanying her to the Portuguese court, and perhaps it was a
mistake on her part to have brought along Inês de Castro, described

OPPOSITE
*Inês de Castro, the daughter
of an illegitimate grandson
of King Sancho IV of
Castile, was well-bred and
renowned for her beauty
and elegance.*

– 23 –

> "*Inês was as beautiful as a flower, blond as the sun, and extremely elegant*"

by a chronicler of the day as being as "beautiful as a flower, blond as the sun, and extremely elegant." For Peter it was love at first sight, and so he was bitterly disappointed when introduced to the real Constance, a brunette of undistinguished appearance. Peter had already rejected one match his father advocated on the grounds that the girl in question was not attractive enough, so Afonso IV had been careful not to let him see a portrait of Constance before her arrival in Lisbon lest he reject this match too. His plan backfired, though, as before long Peter began an all-consuming love affair with Inês that threatened to rip the kingdom of Portugal right down the middle and start an all-out war with Castile.

FORBIDDEN LOVE

Inês de Castro was the illegitimate daughter of an important Galician nobleman and his Portuguese mistress, and the family was well-connected in Castilian royal circles. She was just fifteen when she arrived in Lisbon and stole Peter's heart. It must have been enormously flattering to be wooed by the heir to the throne, although no doubt life was fraught as Constance, her mistress, did her best to separate them. Legend has it that Peter used to send his love letters to Inês through a water pipe connecting the royal estate with the monastery where she lived. He soon found that as well as being beautiful, Inês was a kind, generous woman with a lively wit, and his feelings for her grew ever deeper.

Peter paid little attention to his new wife, so smitten was he with her lady-in-waiting, although he did his stately duty and made Constance pregnant to ensure that there would be an heir to the throne. Their son, Luis, was born in February 1340, and, in an attempt to put an end to the humiliating love affair, Constance asked Inês to be his godmother. In the eyes of the Catholic Church this made Inês a member of the family and her relationship with Peter was therefore considered incestuous. However, Constance's scheme was foiled when the baby died at just a few weeks old, leaving Peter and Inês free to resume their affair.

Peter's father, King Afonso IV, strongly disapproved of the romance, and, to Peter's dismay, he ordered that Inês be expelled from the country. She was sent to Castile in 1344 and installed in a castle there. Far from forgetting her, Peter wrote long passionate letters full of love and poetry, and he rode over to visit her regularly. Afonso's plan to separate them was not working.

In 1345, poor Constance died two weeks after giving birth to her third child, Ferdinand, Peter's son and heir. Immediately, Peter brought Inês back to Lisbon and installed her in the monastery of Santa Clara in the town of Coimbra. They were able to live together as man and wife in a nearby house, but he hoped that the monastery would provide her with protection when he was not around. The two were more in love than ever, and over the next ten years had four children together, one of whom died in infancy. Inês's brothers became close friends and advisors to Peter, and they began trying to persuade him to lay claim to the throne of Castile after the death of Alfonso XI, when the line of succession was unclear because of all the illegitimate children he had sired. King Afonso tried desperately to arrange another marriage for Peter, but his son refused all candidates. He just wanted to be with Inês.

When Peter gave in to the persuasion of the de Castros and declared himself a candidate for the throne of Castile, it was the final straw. King Afonso knew that his actions could drag Portugal into a long and costly war with her neighbors. He was also worried because Inês and Peter I's surviving children, Beatriz, Joao, and Dinis, were strong and healthy, while Prince Ferdinand was weak, and he feared that one day they might attempt to claim the Portuguese throne. The de Castros might even

ABOVE
*Peter I of Portugal,
c. 1632. He was by most
accounts a good and fair
king, who protected his
poorest subjects—but he
completely lost his head
over Inês de Castro.*

try to kill Ferdinand. After long discussions with his advisors, Afonso decided that the only solution was to get Inês out of the way. In January 1355, at a time when he knew Peter was away from home hunting, King Afonso rode to Coimbra with three courtiers, Pêro Coelho, Âlvaro Gonçalves and Diogo Lopes Pacheco. When they arrived at the monastery, Inês immediately realized their intent and surrounded herself with her children, pleading with Afonso not to kill the mother of his own grandchildren. Her only crime, she said, had been her love for his son Peter.

Looking down at the children's innocent faces, Afonso struggled with his conscience. Eventually, unable to give the order personally, he left the room, saying to his courtiers, "Do whatever you want." They opted to carry out his initial orders and brutally stabbed Inês while her children watched and, according to contemporary accounts, screamed and clung to her dying body. It was said that her blood stained the stone bed of a spring red as she uttered her final cry.

THE YOUNG PRETENDERS

There was a good reason for kings not to go around siring illegitimate children all over the land, because at any moment the offspring or their descendants could turn up and try to claim the throne. Peter was only able to make a bid for the throne of Castile in 1354 because of the number of bastards Alfonso XI had left behind, who watered down the rights of succession. After Peter's son Ferdinand died in 1383 without leaving a male successor, Inês de Castro's sons Joao and Dinis both made unsuccessful bids for the throne; it was eventually won by John, the son Peter later had with Teresa Lourenço. Those who make a claim for a throne, whether legitimate or illegitimate, are known as "pretenders." France has two main families of pretenders to this day: the Dukes of Anjou, who trace their ancestors back to Hugh Capet in the 10th century, and the Counts of Paris, descendants of King Louis-Philippe (1830–48). In Britain, the name "The Young Pretender" is given to Bonnie Prince Charlie, grandson of James II, who led an unsuccessful uprising in 1745. And there are many pretenders to the throne of 21st-century Russia due to complexities in the rules of succession of the Romanov dynasty.

RIGHT
Bonnie Prince Charlie, who led an uprising in 1745 in an attempt to restore his family to the throne, was defeated at the Battle of Culloden.

BLOODTHIRSTY REVENGE

Peter was devastated when he returned home to find his beautiful Inês murdered. His overwhelming grief soon turned to white-hot fury and he staged a revolt against his father with the help of the de Castro brothers. For several months, his troops swept through the Portuguese countryside and then laid siege to the city of Porto. His mother pleaded with him to desist until finally she managed to negotiate a fragile reconciliation between father and son. Peter returned to the fold, promising to let bygones be bygones. But he lied.

Two years later, when King Afonso IV died and Peter succeeded to the throne, one of his first priorities was to hunt down the men who had killed Inês. Two of them were hiding in Castile, but Peter negotiated a swap for some Castilian fugitives who were hiding in Portugal and had them brought back. Once there, it is said Peter tried them, found them guilty, then had them executed in particularly barbaric fashion. One's heart was ripped out through his chest and the other's was ripped out through his back, both while they were still alive. Peter watched the scene while eating his dinner and, according to legend, the still-beating hearts were brought to him on a tray and he bit into them. The third assassin, Diogo Lopes Pacheco, had escaped to France, but it's said he had a heart attack and died after hearing the fate of his comrades.

FERDINANDVS PRIMVS LVSITANIÆ REX IX.

All Peter's advisors urged him to take another wife but he refused.
He had a mistress, Teresa Lourenço, the daughter of a Lisbon
merchant, with whom he had a son John, but no one could ever
take Inês's place in his heart. On June 12, 1360, five years after her
death, Peter announced to the country that he and Inês had married
in secret in Bragança. The Bishop of Guarda and one of his servants
corroborated the story (although when you are a king, it's not difficult
to find people who will say what you want them to say). No written
evidence survives of the marriage and it was not recognized by the
Catholic Church in Rome, but Peter was insistent that they had wed,
if somewhat unsure of the date.

Peter had Inês officially declared his legitimate wife and therefore
the lawful queen of Portugal. He ordered
the construction of two magnificent
sarcophagi at the royal monastery in
Alcobaça where he and his love would
one day lie foot to foot so that on the
Day of Judgment, when all souls rose
up from the dead, the first thing they
would see would be each other's faces.

> *Peter was insistent that
> they had wed, if somewhat
> unsure of the date*

Peter obsessed over the tiny details of every inscription on the white marble tomb, and had effigies of Inês's assassins carved to support it so that they would symbolically bear the weight of their sin forever. Next he had her body exhumed from its grave in the monastery of Santa Clara in Coimbra and carried to Alcobaça amidst a procession of noblemen, maids, and clergymen on horseback. Local people came out to marvel at the sight as a thousand men surrounded the procession holding candles that burned at all hours of day and night. According to a contemporary source, "Inês de Castro was led to Alcobaça between two lines of stars."

QUEEN AFTER DEATH

When the procession arrived in Alcobaça on April 2, 1361, according to a royal chronicler, Peter was consumed by "a great madness." He dressed Inês's remains in rich robes and jewels and placed them on the throne next to his. Next he placed the royal crown on her head and insisted that all the nobles of the court and members of the clergy came up in turn to swear allegiance and kiss the queen's hand. Since she had been dead for more than six years, this must have been a rather grisly and unpleasant duty. Only after everyone had paid

BELOW
Resting in the tomb of the kings in the Monastery of Alcobaça: at Peter's insistence the statue of Inês on top of her white marble sarcophagus wears a crown.

INÊS DE CASTRO REMEMBERED

The story of Inês and Peter quickly became lore in Portugal, and in succeeding centuries it went on to inspire poets, dramatists, artists, and composers all around the Western world. There have been dozens of operas and ballets about her, by composers from the UK, US, Canada, Switzerland, Germany, and Italy as well as Portugal and Spain. The 1652 Spanish play *Reinar después de morir (Reign after Death)* by Luis Vélez de Guevara and the 1942 French play *La reine morte (The Dead Queen)* by Henri de Montherlant are among dramas about her that are still revived. And in the 20th century, the deathly figure of Inês crops up several times in *The Cantos* by Ezra Pound, written between 1916 and 1962. The first film about her came out in 1910, a silent movie entitled *Inês de Castro: Rainha depois de Morta (Queen after Death)*, and more have followed, including one by José Carlos de Oliveira in 1997 called *Inês de Portugal*. It is still possible to visit the Quinta das Lágrimas (House of Tears) in Coimbra, where Inês's blood reputedly stained the stones in the spring red, and to view the sarcophagi in Alcobaça. The story of their love affair is the Portuguese version of Romeo and Juliet: romantic, haunting, and desperately tragic.

homage did he allow the great love of his life to be placed in her tomb to wait until they could be reunited once more.

History may remember the bloodthirsty way in which Peter dispatched Inês's killers, but it was not particularly extreme by the standards of justice of the day. In fact, he won himself a reputation as a good and fair king. He curbed the excesses of the nobility and took steps to protect the common people from them, earning himself the nickname "Peter the Just." Admittedly, some of his nobles called him "Peter the Cruel," but only those who held a grudge against him. When he died in 1367, Ferdinand, the son he'd had with Constance, took the throne but he would be the last member of that dynasty to rule. After a succession crisis during the years 1383–85, Peter's son John took the throne, then in 1433, John's son Edward succeeded him. The new King Edward was already married to Eleanor of Aragon, a great-great granddaughter of Inês de Castro, so subsequent kings of Portugal were descended from both her and Peter I after all. Their tombs still face each other in the monastery of Alcobaça, symbolizing a love that no one and nothing could stifle: not separation, royal command, nor even death itself.

ABOVE
Of the many operas based on the tragic story of Peter and Inês, this one, by Giuseppe Persiani from a libretto by Salvadore Cammarano, was first presented at La Scala in January 1837. It was so popular, there were sixty more productions over the next sixteen years.

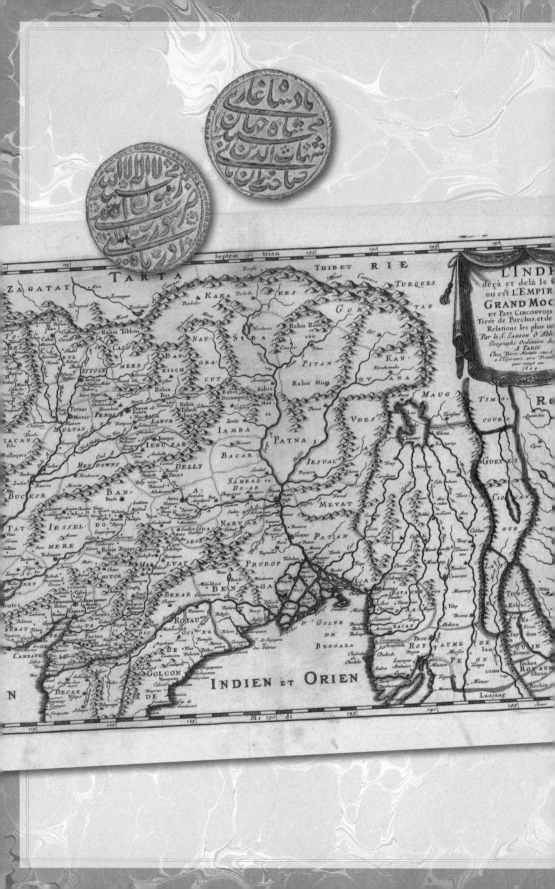

Shah Jahan
– & –
Mumtaz Mahal

**A'la Azad abul Muzaffar Shahab ud–Din
Mohammad Khurram
(Prince Khurram, later Shah Jahan)**
*Born: January 5, 1592, Lahore, Mughal Empire
Died: February 1, 1666, Agra, India*

Arjumand Banu (later Mumtaz Mahal)
*Born: April 6, 1593, Agra, Mughal Empire
Died: June 17, 1631, Burhanpur, India*

Married: May 10, 1612

In an age when polygamy was the norm and men who loved just one woman were seen as weak, the young Prince Khurram, who would later become Shah Jahan, fell for Arjumand Banu with every fiber of his being and was determined not to be parted from her for a single day.

rjumand Banu's grandfather, Ghiyas Beg, was a Persian aristocrat who traveled to the Mughal Court in 1577 in search of advancement. His family was robbed on the way and arrived penniless, but Beg was a clever man and got work as a court official, soon rising to the position of chief minister to Emperor Jahangir. The family was ambitious and well-educated and they thrived in Agra (now a city in northern India), where Persians were admired as being artistically talented and intellectual. Noblewomen were veiled and lived in a sheltered harem, where the only men to see them were their husbands or the eunuchs who served them. However, there was one occasion in the year when women might mingle with men and that was the Royal Meena Bazaar, which took place during the Nowruz or New Year festival. For eighteen days while this fair continued by night among trees hung with colored lanterns, women could browse through stalls where traders sold silver trinkets and lengths of brightly colored silk. It was here that fifteen-year-old Prince Khurram first caught sight of the fourteen-year-old Arjumand Banu, said to be exceptionally beautiful beyond all other women. As was the custom, she wore a silken veil across her face so only the eyes were visible, but this festival was one of the few times when women were allowed to drop their veils briefly and show their faces. When Prince Khurram saw Arjumand Banu's beauty, his affections were won and in April 1607 they were betrothed.

It would be five years before their wedding could go ahead, though. The first obstacle to their happiness came when

OPPOSITE
According to courtiers, the "intimacy and deep affection" Shah Jahan and Mumtaz had for each other "was not merely out of carnal desire but high virtues and pleasing habits, outward and inward goodness, and physical and spiritual compatibility on both sides."

BELOW
Prince Khurram was an abstemious man—he drank "only during festivals and on cloudy days," and in 1620 gave up wine altogether.

Ghiyas Beg was accused of corruption and then of plotting with his sons to kill the Emperor. He bribed his way out of danger but one of his sons was executed for his part in the conspiracy. Meanwhile, Prince Khurram was ordered by his father to marry a Persian princess named Shah Ismail Safavi—he had no choice but to obey because only through marriage would he achieve official manhood—and in 1611 she bore him a daughter. It must have been hard for Arjumand Banu to hear of his marriage. The Koran permitted men to take up to four main wives and any number of supposedly second-tier wives, but still she would surely have wished to be his first. In the same year perhaps her hopes were raised when her Aunt Mehrunissa married the Emperor and the family fortunes began to improve. At last, on May 10, 1612, a date that the court astrologers guaranteed was auspicious and would bring them great happiness, Arjumand Banu and Prince Khurram were wed.

The wedding ceremonials were lavish. Prince Khurram's hands were painted with henna and turmeric for luck and a tiara of pearls was tied around his head. Gifts exchanged between the two families were described as "costly products of mines and quarries and the choicest harvest of the Garden of Eden." Prince Khurram drank a goblet of water to confirm the marriage, then the feast took place at the bride's father's house, with fireworks and elaborate processions continuing over the next month.

On their wedding night, the couple were bathed, perfumed with oils, and placed on a huge bed, where servants caressed them to arouse them. At the age of twenty, Prince Khurram was said to have been very experienced in the art of love-making. The people of India were renowned for their sensuality and their prowess in varied sexual techniques, and according to the imperial chroniclers, Prince Khurram had especially strong sexual appetites. The morning after the wedding, the bedsheets were examined to confirm that coitus had taken place and that Arjumand had been a virgin. Six weeks later, she was pregnant with their first child.

THE PERFECT WIFE

According to the chroniclers, Prince Khurram was dazzled by his new wife's beauty and found her to be "chief and elect [*mumtaz*] from among the women of the time and the ladies of the universe." He gave her the name Mumtaz Mahal Bega, which was a great honor for her and clearly set her above the other wife he had taken, whom he no longer visited. According to court chroniclers, "his whole delight was centered in this illustrious lady." They lived in a palace on the Jumna River in Agra, where she had an apartment within the harem to which Prince Khurram came every evening. He was faithful, unlike his father who enjoyed a variety of sexual partners and was said to have bedded over three hundred women.

In 1614, shortly after Mumtaz gave birth to a baby girl, the Emperor ordered Prince Khurram to travel to Mewar (Udaipur) to subdue a rebellion by the Rana. Khurram insisted that Mumtaz come with him even though she had a new baby and was already pregnant again, setting a pattern they would follow for the rest of their married life: "he never allowed that light of the imperial chamber to be separated from him whether at home or abroad." Whenever his father sent him to some far-flung stretch of the kingdom, Mumtaz and the royal household would come, too, the ladies traveling in sedan chairs carried by servants or in a howdah on an elephant's back. It was slow progress; they generally only covered about ten miles a day before they stopped and servants set about pitching an elaborate camp where they would dine and spend the night.

For the first seven years of their marriage, Mumtaz gave birth to a child a year—a feat that made her contemporaries marvel. She mourned after a daughter died of smallpox in 1616, and when a son who had been frail from birth died in 1622, but as a good royal wife, she provided plenty of heirs for her husband. She must have been distraught when the Emperor insisted that Prince Khurram marry another wife, the granddaughter of his

ABOVE
Shah Jahan led his men the length and breadth of the kingdom quelling uprisings, always accompanied by his beloved wife.

commander-in-chief, on the exact day that Mumtaz gave birth to their fifth child in 1617. She would have been even more upset when her husband went on to father a son with this new bride, but the court historians are clear that it was a marriage of political expediency and that the "illustrious connection" was in name only. The child of this new marriage died in his first year.

Prince Khurram had gained a reputation as a clever diplomat and a skilled tactician and was rewarded by his father with many gifts, including the governorship of Gujarat, a special throne in the Durbar (the Mughal court), and the title of "Shah Jahan," meaning "Lord of the World." All this was significant because it positioned him as the most worthy candidate to succeed his father in due course, better placed than his half-brother Khusrau or any other close relatives. However, he had reckoned without the increasing influence of the Emperor's wife, Mehrunissa, known as Nur. She enjoyed her power in court and didn't want Shah Jahan to succeed. She began scheming against him, dropping poisonous words into his father's ear while he was off fighting military campaigns.

In January 1622, word came that Prince Khusrau had died in the fortress of Burhanpur, in central India, and a rumor began to spread that Shah Jahan had ordered his murder. Relations with his father became so strained that he decided the time had come to openly rebel against the Emperor. He was thirty years old and wanted to secure his own future rather than risk it being undermined by Nur, the ambitious new wife. There followed a difficult three years when Shah Jahan, Mumtaz, and their young children traveled thousands of miles around the kingdom, fleeing the Emperor's armies and trying to raise support for their own campaign. Ultimately the rebellion failed because the old Emperor's armies were too strong, but in October 1627, when Jahangir died, Shah Jahan was determined not to let the throne slip through his fingers. In one fell swoop he had his remaining half-brother, two nephews, and two cousins killed so that there could be no further rivals for the throne. He imprisoned his stepmother Nur, and on February 14, 1628, he achieved his ambition and became ruler of the Mughal Empire.

OPPOSITE
The fabulous Peacock Throne commissioned by Shah Jahan was captured in 1739 by Persian leader Nader Shah, and has never been recovered.

THREE BLESSED YEARS

After so many years on the run, Shah Jahan was determined to live in luxury, so he and his wife established themselves in sumptuous apartments at the Red Fort in Agra. He was a connoisseur of precious

THE ART OF THE MUGHAL EMPIRE

The Mughals came from central Asia and began their rule over the Indian subcontinent in 1526, extending their influence until, under Shah Jahan's son Aurangzeb, they ruled all but the southern tip of India, plus the territory that is now Pakistan and Afghanistan. Emperor Akbar (r. 1556–1605) was interested in painting and set up studios that developed a distinctive style, combining the sophistication and detail of Persian art with the bold colors used by Indian artists. Emperor Jahangir (r. 1605–27) commissioned many miniatures from these studios, depicting animals, birds, and scenes of life in court rather than the military subjects favored by his predecessor. He was also a connoisseur of precious stones, and his royal workshops produced many exquisite objects. Shah Jahan shared his father and grandfather's love of art and jewels, but also took a strong interest in architecture. This culminated in the greatest work he ever had built—his wife's tomb, the Taj Mahal. However, the arts declined under Emperor Aurangzeb and the empire began to fall apart. In 1858 the British abolished the title "Emperor" as they expanded their own empire in the subcontinent.

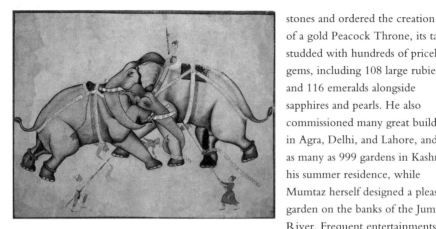

ABOVE
Elephant fights were a favorite spectacle in the Mughal court. Riders goaded the elephants until they had sufficiently enraged them, then leaped clear as the mighty animals charged at each other.

stones and ordered the creation of a gold Peacock Throne, its tail studded with hundreds of priceless gems, including 108 large rubies and 116 emeralds alongside sapphires and pearls. He also commissioned many great buildings in Agra, Delhi, and Lahore, and as many as 999 gardens in Kashmir, his summer residence, while Mumtaz herself designed a pleasure garden on the banks of the Jumna River. Frequent entertainments were presented for the court, including singers, dancers, and musicians, as well as elephant fights.

Every day, Shah Jahan ate his meals in the harem with Mumtaz, and they spent the evenings together listening to music, playing chess, or making love. He often discussed affairs of state with her and trusted her with a royal seal, giving her the right to issue her own orders and make appointments to official positions. She was a woman of good sense and a pleasant nature who didn't seek to wield power in the same way as her predecessor Nur had done, but was content simply to support her beloved husband. A court poet wrote: "No dust from her behavior ever settled/On the mirror of the Emperor's mind."

> *"No dust from her behavior ever settled on the mirror of the Emperor's mind"*

Mumtaz remained beautiful in her late thirties, even after giving birth to twelve children. She used concoctions made from plants, seeds, and oils to care for her skin and hair, kohl to line her eyes, and she would have used pastes and liniments to keep her vaginal muscles in good shape for lovemaking. She dressed in robes of fine, flowing fabrics in gorgeous shades, wore a turban with an ostrich plume on her head, and always accessorized with fabulous jewelry, given as gifts by her doting husband.

It was an idyllic life but it was not to last. In late 1629, when Mumtaz was heavily pregnant with her thirteenth child, Shah Jahan had to march south against a rebellious sultan and, as usual, he took his wife along. Soon after their arrival at Burhanpur in 1630, the child was born but died shortly thereafter. Before long, Mumtaz was pregnant again. She hoped to return to Agra, where she was planning the marriage of her eldest son, fifteen-year-old Dara Shukoh, but Shah Jahan could not leave the south. In June 1631, Mumtaz went into labor and those attending her reported hearing something very odd: the baby crying out from within the womb. Everyone took this as an ill omen. The labor lasted for thirty hours and with each hour that passed Mumtaz lost more blood and became weaker and weaker.

In despair, she sent for Shah Jahan and told him that this was their time of separation. She made him promise not to have children with any other women after she was gone, but instead, to look after their own living children, of whom there were now seven. She told her husband she had dreamed of "a beautiful palace with a lush garden, the like of which she had never imagined," and her parting words were "Build for me a mausoleum which would be unique, extremely beautiful, the like of which is not on earth." And then, according to the chroniclers, "when three watches of the said night still remained . . . she passed on to God."

For nineteen years, Mumtaz had been "the light of his bedchamber," from whom he could not bear to be parted, and Shah Jahan fell apart upon her death. In his grief he even considered renouncing the throne. His eyes were so reddened "from constant weeping that he was forced to use spectacles," and he went into deep mourning, from which he emerged two years later with white hair, a bent back and a face worn by grief. The only thing he could do for Mumtaz now was to fulfill her dying wish and build her a mausoleum that would be greater than any other ever known to the world. He chose a site that could be

BELOW
The Red Fort at Agra. A fort has stood on the site since 1080, but in the years 1565–73 the Mughals erected the world-famous elaborate red sandstone building as a secure home for the royal family.

The Delhi Gate - Agra Fort

THE TAJ MAHAL

The world's most exquisite mausoleum is constructed from white marble and set in a walled garden with a long white marble pool designed to reflect the main building in its waters. The dome and flanking minarets are a distinctive image recognized around the world as a symbol of love. The building is covered by carvings and stucco, representing flowers (the iris, lily, lotus, and tulip), abstract Islamic patterns, and calligraphy of quotations from the Koran or from Persian poems. The chief calligrapher Amanat Khan was so skilled that Shah Jahan allowed him to be the only person who inscribed his name on his work. The interior chamber of the Taj is decorated with precious and semi-precious stones of great value, reflecting Shah Jahan's connoisseurship. In the gardens outside, fountains play, goldfish swim in the ponds, and luxuriant trees and flowers blossom. Everything is perfectly symmetrical, displaying the architects' profound knowledge of mathematics. Some experts believe that Shah Jahan planned to build himself a corresponding "black Taj" for his final resting place, but was prevented from doing so by his son.

seen from his apartments in Agra's Red Fort, and the work began on a magnificent building he named the Taj Mahal ("Taj" being short for Mumtaz), a tribute to the woman who had been his one true love. He was intimately involved in the design and planning of the great mausoleum, personally approving every last stone during the twenty years of its construction.

Shah Jahan's only comfort during this time was his eldest daughter Jahanara, to whom he became

so close that there were rumors of incest, though this seems unlikely. His sexual needs were taken care of by scores of different conquests picked up at the Meena Bazaar, but he was careful to respect Mumtaz's dying wish that he should not have children with any of them. He no longer paid attention to the running of his kingdom, leaving it to his sons and military commanders, and in his final years his son Aurangzeb imprisoned him in the Red Fort so that he couldn't interfere after Aurangzeb declared himself emperor. Shah Jahan died on a balcony looking out toward the Taj Mahal where his beloved wife's body lay, and after death he was laid to rest beside her for eternity.

BELOW
The world's ultimate symbol of undying love. Building the Taj Mahal was the only thing that kept Shah Jahan going during the grief-stricken years after Mumtaz's death.

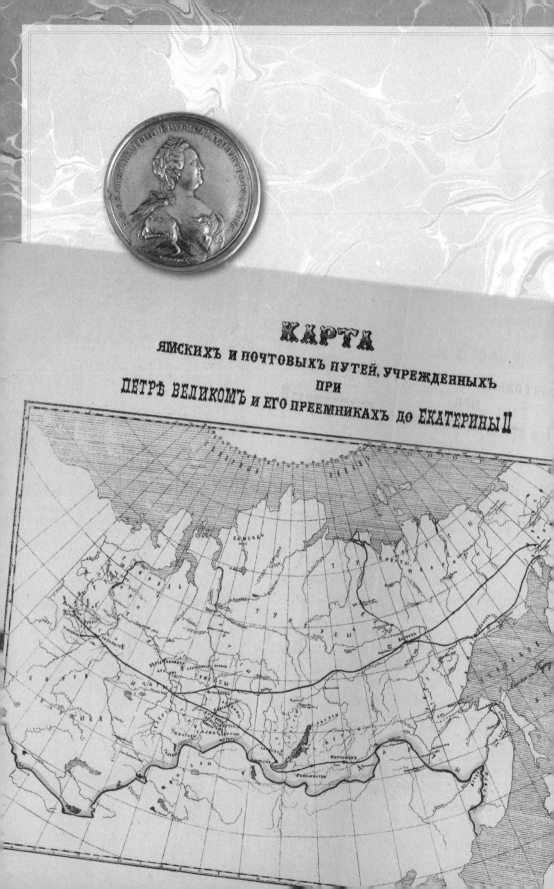

КАРТА

ЯМСКИХЪ И ПОЧТОВЫХЪ ПУТЕЙ, УЧРЕЖДЕННЫХЪ

при

ПЕТРѢ ВЕЛИКОМЪ И ЕГО ПРЕЕМНИКАХЪ до ЕКАТЕРИНЫ II

Catherine the Great
– & –
Grigory Potemkin

**Sophia Friederike Auguste
(later Catherine Alexeyevna)**
Born: May 2, 1729, Stettin, Pomerania, Germany
Died: November 17, 1796, St. Petersburg, Russia

Grigory Alexandrovich Potemkin–Tavricheski
Born: October 11, 1739, Chizhovo, Russia
Died: October 16, 1791, Jassy, Moldavia

Married: possibly June 9, 1774

—◦❀◦—

Catherine was an intelligent woman who proved a shrewd ruler of Russia, but she yearned for a man by her side. Not many were up to the role, but in military commander Grigory Potemkin she found her soul mate.

—◦❀◦—

Catherine was born Princess Sophia of the German principality of Anhalt-Zerbst, but it was a minor princely house and her family was not particularly wealthy or powerful. She had an uneventful childhood, educated by a French governess and a succession of tutors. While she was in her early teens, a marriage was arranged with her second cousin Peter, heir to the throne of Russia, as a means of strengthening the bond between Prussia and Russia and lessening Austrian influence in the Tsarist court. Sophia disliked Peter on first meeting, later noting in her memoirs that she found him an "idiot" and a "drunkard," but she was a determined character and decided to make the best of her situation. She was accepted into the Orthodox faith in June 1744 and given the new name of Catherine Alexeyevna. In August the following year she was married in St. Petersburg at the age of just sixteen years. It did not augur well when her new husband failed to come to her bedchamber on their wedding night and as the months went by showed no sign of wanting to consummate the marriage. Catherine applied herself to learning the Russian language and making friends in the foreign court, keen to prove herself worthy of the crown she would one day wear.

By the early 1750s, when Peter had still not come to Catherine's bed, she had begun a string of flirtations and taken her first lover, Sergei Saltykov, a chamberlain in their palace at Oranienbaum. Her child Paul, born on September 20, 1754, was almost certainly Saltykov's son, but was whisked away from her by the Empress

OPPOSITE
Catherine and Peter. History books tend to portray him unkindly, with the 1911 Encyclopedia Britannica saying, "Nature had made him mean, the smallpox had made him hideous, and his degraded habits made him loathsome," but this view is largely drawn from Catherine's memoirs, so is undoubtedly biased.

BELOW
Sergei Saltykov, c. 1750. According to Catherine, he was "handsome as the dawn" and she took him as a lover, probably her first.

Elizabeth, Peter's mother, to be brought up as heir to the throne. This was standard practice for an heir, but it left her in tears, feeling "cruelly abandoned." In 1755, Catherine met Polish noble Stanislas Poniatowski and fell madly in love. He fathered her second child, a daughter called Anna, born in 1757, who was once again whisked away by her mother-in-law. Catherine's next lover, Grigory Orlov, was a lieutenant in the Ismailovsky Guards, a tall, charming man who swept her off her feet. By taking lovers in this way, Catherine was not being unduly promiscuous by the standards of the Russian court of the day. Later accounts would attempt to blacken her name and paint her as an insatiable nymphomaniac, but the truth was that she liked male company, she liked sex, and ultimately she was seeking someone

RIGHT
An 1861 engraving showing Catherine at the head of her army. She was aware that the army had won her the crown and the army could take it away again. "The least soldier of the Guard thinks when he sees me, 'That is the work of my hands,'" she wrote in her diary.

who could fulfil her emotional needs. She fell in love with each of her lovers, and was frequently heartbroken when they were unwilling to provide the level of devotion she required.

> *He cracked a joke that made Catherine laugh. He had been noticed*

In December 1761, Empress Elizabeth died and Peter came to the throne, but before long he had made enemies in all the wrong places. He behaved disrespectfully at his mother's funeral, seized lands belonging to the Orthodox Church, pursued unwise foreign policy, and outraged the royal guards. Catherine was disgusted by his behavior and welcomed it when her lover Orlov, along with his brothers, planned a coup to put her on the throne. But she was pregnant with her third child (probably Orlov's), so they had to wait until after she had given birth, in April 1762.

Finally, one night at the end of June, Catherine, dressed in a green guards uniform to confirm her role as head of the troops, led the conspirators on horseback against her husband. She was holding a saber and, so the story goes, a young guardsman named Grigory Potemkin noticed that she did not have a dragonne or sword knot on it, so rode up to give her his own. After handing it over, he bowed and pulled on the reins, but at first his horse would not move away and he cracked a joke that made Catherine laugh. He had been noticed.

The following day Peter III was forced to abdicate and on July 5 he was murdered by Grigory Orlov's brother Alexei. The way was clear for Catherine to take the throne of Russia. In dispatches, she praised "a subaltern of seventeen named Potemkin" for his "discernment, courage, and action." In fact, Grigory Potemkin was 23 years old to Catherine's 33, and it wouldn't be long before he caught her attention again.

ENTERTAINING THE EMPRESS

Catherine was crowned Empress of Russia on September 22, 1762, and had soon employed Potemkin as a member of her royal household. He was a witty man, renowned for being an excellent mimic, and when Catherine heard this, she invited him to do an impression. The court fell silent as he began to mimic Catherine herself. Nobles were unsure how to react until she threw back her head and roared with laughter; he'd got away with it. Potemkin's duties included standing behind Catherine's chair at mealtimes to serve her, and they often engaged in conversation. It wasn't long before Potemkin had

fallen passionately in love with her and took the dangerous step of getting down on his knees to proclaim his feelings. Catherine had many suitors, and was still ensconced in her affair with Grigory Orlov, but she humored him and evidently enjoyed the company of this lively, forceful personality.

Potemkin came from Chizhova, near Smolensk, on the western fringes of the Russian empire. His father had died when he was six, but he was groomed for military service by his godfather and won a place at a renowned school before going on to study at Moscow University. He was well over six feet tall, handsome, funny, and very attractive to women, although he also had a reputation for drinking, gambling, and louche behavior that made his family despair. His charm and intelligence led to his rapid promotion in the army, and he remained a captain in the guards even after taking up his position in the royal household. It must have crossed Potemkin's mind that being picked to be one of the Empress's lovers would be a smart career move, as she showered her favorites with generous gifts and appointed them to prestigious jobs, but when he got to know her it seems he genuinely fell for her. Italian lothario Casanova described Catherine thus: "Though not beautiful, she was sure to please by her sweetness, affability and her intelligence." And Poniatowski, her old lover, spoke of her "expressive blue eyes . . . kissable mouth . . . agreeable voice and a gay good-tempered laugh."

From the start, Catherine proved a wise ruler of Russia, dealing ruthlessly but fairly with her enemies and picking the right men to run the country. She began to favor Potemkin, charting a career in government for him, but she merely laughed it off when he declared his love because she was still involved with Grigory Orlov. Orlov took it seriously, though. Some time in 1763, according to legend, Potemkin was invited to play a game of billiards with Alexei Orlov, the brother who had previously murdered the Emperor, Peter. When Potemkin arrived, Alexei beat him up so badly that he lost his left eye. Potemkin immediately left the court, sure that Catherine would despise him now he had been so grievously disfigured. He stopped making any effort with his appearance, and over the next eighteen months he became unkempt, fell into a deep depression, and took to studying religion. Catherine missed his company and wrote to him "It is a great pity that a person of such rare merits is lost from society." At last she persuaded him to return to court and promoted him to new positions of power—but still she took Orlov to her bed.

When a Russo-Turkish war began in September 1768, Potemkin requested that he might serve there and he acquitted himself well at the front. He and Catherine began to correspond with each other and when he returned a war hero in 1771, it was clear they were becoming closer. She often asked his advice and invited him to dine with her, but still she wouldn't take him into her bed. She had broken off the relationship with Orlov because of his infidelities, but had a new lover, Vassilchikov. At last, in January 1774, Potemkin forced her hand by moving into the Alexander Nevsky monastery claiming he was going to

LEFT
A 1792 cartoon shows Catherine with bared chest stepping from Russia into Constantinople to the south, while other European rulers look up her skirt. This was typical of the way she was portrayed as a powerful woman but one with loose morals.

take holy orders. He was pretty sure Catherine was attracted to him and that she would miss him when he was gone. Sure enough, she instantly dispatched one of her ladies-in-waiting to bring him back and after a courtship of thirteen years he finally became the Empress's lover.

AN ALL-CONSUMING LOVE

What a passion it was! Potemkin moved into luxurious apartments in the Winter Palace, connected to Catherine's rooms by a corridor, so he was able to wander into her bedchamber at will. They often met in the palace banya (the baths), and if they were separated for more than an hour during the day they wrote love letters to each other. She described him as "one of the greatest, wittiest and most original eccentrics of this iron century." The eccentric description was one few would deny who encountered him lying on sofas wrapped in a half-open bearskin with a pink bandana round his head. He was sexually experienced, he made her laugh, and possessed an intelligence to match her own, but it was a stormy relationship. He was jealous of her past lovers and didn't like to take orders, so sometimes he withdrew, leaving her feeling insecure and possessive. "If you wish to keep me for ever," she wrote, "show as much friendship as affection and continue to love me and to tell me the truth."

That she loved Potemkin above all others is clear, and some historians are convinced that they slipped off and married secretly in June 1774 (the night of June 8/9 is suspected). A letter from Catherine refers to their secret enterprise that night and afterwards she signed her letters to him, "devoted wife," and called him "dear husband." "I am bound to you by all possible ties," she wrote, and referred to the two of them as "twin souls." During the summer of 1774, Potemkin and Catherine honeymooned in a cottage on the Tsaritsyno estate and there was gossip

BELOW
The palaces of the tsars in St. Petersburg line the shores of the Baltic. This panoramic view was drawn by J.A. Atkinson for Catherine's grandson, Alexander I.

that she was pregnant with his child but, at the age of 45, it seems unlikely. Certainly no child ever appeared. Regardless, Potemkin's position was secure. From then on, he was treated as a member of the imperial family, with access to both the Russian treasury and Catherine's innermost thoughts, a state of affairs that remained the case for the rest of his life.

PASSION SUBSIDES BUT LOVE REMAINS

By the end of 1775, cracks were beginning to show in the relationship. Potemkin resented his subordinate position and sometimes pleaded illness when summoned to her bedchamber. Loving her was a full-time job and no man could keep her happy without losing his self-respect, because she demanded complete and utter commitment. They had furious quarrels but, as Catherine wrote, "The essence of our disagreement is always the question of power and never that of love."

In January 1776, a new young secretary, Peter Zadovsky, came to work for Catherine; Potemkin, feeling it would ease pressure on him, encouraged her to take Peter as her lover, although it seems she still slept with Potemkin as well. Around this time, she asked Joseph II to make Potemkin a Prince of the Holy Roman Empire, and in this way he became first governor-general of the southern provinces then president of the colleges of war, roles that would secure his future. She gave him whatever he asked for—houses, wealth, and position—until he had unprecedented power over the country. On the whole he used it wisely, expanding Catherine's empire and bringing stability. Among other achievements, he colonized the Steppes and created several new towns, including Nikolayev and Sevastopol. He reformed the army, built a fleet on the Black Sea, conquered the Crimean peninsula, and was victorious in the second Russo-Turkish War. At home, he built the Tauride Palace in St. Petersburg and advised Catherine on both domestic and foreign

SECRET MARRIAGES

It was only in the 18th century that royal marriages became affairs of state requiring the permission of the reigning monarch. Before then they could be rather more casual, and bigamy was not uncommon. Edward IV of England secretly married the widowed Elizabeth Woodville at her family home in May 1464, and he kept the secret for five months while discussions continued about possibly bringing a bride over from France. However, it may be that Edward had something of a penchant for secret marriages and that he had previously married Lady Eleanor Talbot, who was still alive but had retired to a convent. The succession to the English throne could have been quite different had this ever been proved. In Russia in 1742, the Empress Elizabeth, mother of Peter III, is said to have secretly married her lover Alexei Razumovsky, who became known among his contemporaries as "Emperor of the Night." Back in Britain, in 1785 Maria Fitzherbert married the Prince of Wales in a secret ceremony, but this was later declared invalid since the permission of the sovereign had not been sought. Many years later the Pope decreed their marriage was valid after all, but still she never became queen.

*Catherine loved Potemkin
to distraction. "What a trick
you have played to unbalance
a mind, previously thought
to be one of the best in
Europe," she wrote to him.
Nothing he did could shake
her view that he was the
best of men.*

policy. They corresponded constantly on matters of state as well as affairs of the heart, often gossiping about mutual acquaintances using their own personal nicknames for them. She trusted him absolutely, in a way she trusted no one else, and together they made a formidable team.

Their relationship changed over the years. Catherine took young lovers, usually chosen from Potemkin's staff, with his approval, though none approached the overriding influence he held as her consort, minister, lover, and friend. He was always on hand to discuss her affairs of the heart and advise her on the level of pay-off each lover should receive when his usefulness was at an end. He had dozens of mistresses himself, and it's rumored that he slept with all five of his nieces and may have fallen in love with one of them, a girl named Varvara Engelhardt. (It was not unusual at the time for uncles and nieces to sleep together, but to have slept with all of them was notable.)

In 1791, while Potemkin was in the city of Jassy in the far south of the Empire overseeing peace negotiations with the Turks, he fell ill. Catherine wrote urging him to take care of himself, but before the letter arrived he had passed away. His last words were, "Forgive me, merciful Mother-Sovereign." When news reached the Empress in St. Petersburg, she was distraught. "You cannot imagine how broken I am," she wrote to a confidante. She ordered the entire court into mourning and went into seclusion herself, spending her days writing about Potemkin's magnificent qualities: "he did not betray me, he could not be bought." He had left behind huge debts, but Catherine settled them all. Every day after Potemkin's passing she woke weeping. She no longer had anything to look forward to and the five years before she herself would die of a stroke were tainted with sadness.

It was lonely being a female ruler in a society run by men, especially for a German-born princess wielding power in Russia. Catherine negotiated her tricky position with consummate skill, but inside she yearned for someone to love who would make her feel loved in return, who would be on her side no matter what. In Grigory Potemkin she found that man.

> *She yearned for someone to love who would make her feel loved in return, who would be on her side no matter what*

POSTHUMOUS REPUTATIONS

Catherine's son Paul I succeeded her, and he immediately set about belittling Potemkin's achievements and emphasizing his dissolute lifestyle. Paul popularized a story that Potemkin had built fake villages, mere painted pieces of scenery, to convince visiting officials that he was populating areas of the south, but if such so-called "Potemkin villages" existed, they were few and far between. Throughout the prudish 19th century, when women were not supposed to show so much as a flash of ankle, never mind take lovers, Catherine's sexual appetite was exaggerated to ridiculous extremes; she was portrayed as a sexual predator who indulged in all manner of perversions. It was even said she had her ladies-in-waiting try out her lovers first, then her doctor would test them before they came to the royal bedchamber—a system akin to a sexual production line. All this served for a while to distract attention from the fact that Catherine was a very successful monarch, who supported the arts in her country, built many beautiful mansions, and generally improved the lives of her people. Her reign is now considered to be the Golden Age of the Russian Empire.

Paul I
Emperor of Russia
from a drawing attributed to the Empress
Marie Feodorovna his wife

RIGHT
Paul I, Catherine's son, was not popular and after five years on the throne he was assassinated by a group of nobles as he hid, trembling, behind the curtains in his bedchamber.

Louis XVI
– & –
Marie Antoinette

Louis Auguste de France
Born: August 23, 1754, Versailles, France
Died: January 21, 1793, Paris, France

Maria Antonia Josepha (known as Marie Antoine)
Born: November 2, 1755, Vienna, Austria
Died: October 16, 1793, Paris, France

Married: May 16, 1770

LODEWYK XVI.
Koning van Frankryk en Navarre.

MARIA ANTOINETTA
VAN OOSTENRYK.
Koningin van Frankryk.

Marie Antoine of Austria was just fourteen years old when she was married to fifteen-year-old Louis Auguste of France in a move designed to strengthen the alliance between two countries that had until recently been enemies. She arrived in a foreign land whose people, including her new husband, viewed her with suspicion from the start . . .

Marie Antoine was the fifteenth child of Francis I, Holy Roman Emperor, and his formidable wife, the Empress Maria Theresa. Her childhood was a happy one in the beautiful Palace of Schönbrunn, where each child had a personal suite of five rooms; boys in one wing and girls in another. She wasn't a great scholar but loved music—she heard Mozart play when she was eight years old—and excelled at dancing. It didn't affect her much at the time that between 1754 and 1763 the world was engaged in a war, later known as the Seven Years' War, in which old enemies France and Austria combined forces against Prussia. She didn't know that the French subsequently blamed the Austrians for dragging them into a costly defeat that would later shape her fate.

Marie Antoine's father died just as the war ended and her mother took charge, sharing power with her oldest brother, Joseph. There were complex politics involved in the post-war peace treaties, but Maria Theresa had plenty of children to use as chess pieces in a sophisticated game of marital diplomacy, until in 1767 smallpox hit the family.

OPPOSITE
Louis Auguste was passionate about hunting and kept a detailed journal of his adventures, but when it came to relationships with the opposite sex he was completely out of his depth.

BELOW
Young Marie-Antoine was not considered a great beauty, but her personality was said to be sweet and agreeable.

One sister died; another survived but was too disfigured to marry; a brother and sister had already succumbed to the illness a few years earlier; but Marie Antoine was immune after surviving a bout in childhood. Suddenly she became the best prospect for cementing Austria's newfound alliance with France, and her mother began negotiating for the hand of the heir to the French throne, the Dauphin, Louis Auguste.

Little Marie Antoine had crooked teeth, so her mother insisted she undergo three months of painful treatment with wire braces to straighten them. A hairdresser was brought from Paris to correct her uneven hairline and she was intensively tutored in French, as the complex bargaining continued. There was no question that she would cooperate. As her mother said of her daughters, "They are born to obey and must learn to do so in good time."

At last a dowry of 200,000 florins and jewels worth an equal amount was agreed and the date set. In April 1770 Marie Antoine headed for France, a journey that took two and a half weeks. "Do so much good to the French people that they can say I have sent them an angel," Maria Theresa instructed. Marie Antoine tearfully left behind her family, her country, her pet dog, her Austrian clothes, her native language—and even her name, because she would henceforth be known by the French-style "Marie Antoinette." Many in France were opposed to the match and already there were those who referred to her scornfully as L'Autrichienne (the Austrian woman). She knew she had to be wary of giving them any ammunition.

ABOVE
A portrait of Marie Antoinette. When she sent her daughter to the French court, Maria Theresa pleaded, "Given her age, I pray you to exercise indulgence for any careless mistake."

A UNION OF TWO SHY TEENAGERS

On May 14, 1770, Marie Antoine met her husband-to-be, but if she was disappointed she didn't show it. Louis Auguste was heavily built—plump, some would say—with thick, dark eyebrows and hooded blue eyes. His manner was awkward and clumsy, while Marie Antoinette was very slight and pretty, with an air "at once of grandeur, modesty and sweetness" and "a smile sufficient to win the heart."

Louis Auguste was the third son of the King and had been neglected in childhood since his mother favored his eldest brother, whose standards young Louis was informed he would never attain. He was intelligent and well-educated, but he was not raised to be a king. His hobbies were hunting and metalwork, particularly locksmithing, and he enjoyed reading about history, geography, and astronomy.

But in 1761 Louis Auguste's life changed fundamentally when the death of his older brothers put him in the direct line of succession; after his father's death in 1765, he became the Dauphin of France. He knew his marriage was a matter of political expediency, but listened hard when his tutors warned him that he must not be seen to let his policy be influenced by this new bride of Austria. She must have no power or the people would complain vociferously. This advice led Louis to treat young Marie Antoinette coldly in public so that he would not be seen to favor her, and can hardly have helped her to feel welcome in the French court.

The lavish wedding on May 16, 1770, was followed by the couple's ritual bedding, when King Louis XV helped his grandson

> ## "*Marie Antoinette had a smile sufficient to win the heart*"

THE POUF

When Marie Antoinette arrived at Versailles, there was already a fashion for elaborately dressed and powdered hair, but she took it to new extremes. She started the fashion for tall headdresses known as poufs, created for her by Léonard Autié, a celebrated hairdresser, and the dress designer Rose Bertin. These styles could be several feet tall and adorned with jewels, ostrich feathers, and whatever decoration the wearer desired to suit the occasion. As her subjects copied each new hairstyle, Marie Antoinette took them to ever more absurd extremes. Wire frames supported the shapes, and these could be heavy and cumbersome, making it difficult to get in and out of carriages. The hair could only be washed between styles, and sleep was difficult. During her first pregnancy, Marie Antoinette's hair began to fall out and she was forced to opt for a new, shorter feathery hairstyle, which the ladies of the court instantly copied. And later, having been deposed, in a final irony on the morning of her execution, Léonard Autié came to her cell and roughly cut off her remaining locks in order to leave her neck free for the guillotine's blade.

into bed while the Duchesse de Chartres did the same for Marie Antoinette, watched by high-ranking members of the court. The next morning the sheets were checked and the rumor spread rapidly that the marriage had not been consummated. Marie Antoinette confirmed this in letters to her mother, saying she believed the Dauphin was too shy. Her mother wrote back urging her to inspire his passion. Until the marriage was consummated it could be annulled at any time, putting her daughter in a precarious position. Louis hinted to his bride that perhaps it would happen on his sixteenth birthday, but that date came and went without any resolution. Her mother advised that they should sleep in the same bed every night, but that was not the practice in France. Nonetheless, Louis Auguste gradually warmed to Marie Antoinette, commenting in December 1770, "She has so much grace that she does everything perfectly"—but still he was unable to deflower her.

During the summer of 1772, a doctor's advice was sought and he suggested Louis might be suffering from a condition known as phimosis, for which the cure was circumcision. However, this could have done more harm than good, so Louis hesitated and eventually decided against it. In July 1773, Marie Antoinette wrote to her mother with great joy, announcing that the marriage had at last been consummated. Touchingly, Louis had asked her, "But do you love me?" and she replied that she loved him most sincerely. The two became closer, exchanging tender caresses as well as enjoying nighttime visits, but they waited and waited and still no child was forthcoming. Crude pamphlets known as *libelles*

were circulated in the streets of France asking,
"Can the King do it? Can't the King do it?"

Finally, in April 1777, Marie Antoinette's
eldest brother, the Emperor Joseph, came to
visit and had frank discussions with the royal
couple. It seems that although penetration
had occurred, Louis had not been ejaculating.
Joseph described the pair as "complete
blunderers." His visit made all the difference
and, in 1778, Marie Antoinette gave birth
to her first child—a girl. A son followed in
1781 and was greeted with jubilation in
the court. "Madame, you have fulfilled our
wishes and those of France," Louis told
her, and was so emotional that he cried
throughout the baptism. This first son was
sickly, so it was fortunate that another child
was born in 1785—a strong healthy boy
called Louis Charles. However, by this
time public opinion in France was turning
against L'Autrichienne for her reportedly extravagant ways, and
producing an heir to the throne was not going to be enough to
change their minds.

ABOVE
*The sickly Louis Joseph,
Dauphin of France, with his
older sister Marie Thérèse,
c. 1785. Louis XVI was so
delighted to have a son at
last that he wept all the way
through the baptism, but the
boy died at the age of seven.*

LIFE IN VERSAILLES

Marie Antoinette soon realized that life at the French court at
Versailles was quite different from that at Schönbrunn, with complex
and detailed rules of etiquette governing most areas of life. The wife
of Louis XV, the reigning monarch, had died, so Marie Antoinette
was first lady and thus able to change convention to an extent.
During her first winter, she introduced ice skating to the court only
to quickly drop it after it was declared "too Austrian." She knew she
had to win over the French people and was ecstatic when her first
official visit to Paris, in June 1773, was a success—"the transports of
joy, of affection, that were shown to us," she wrote to her mother.
"How fortunate we are, given our rank, to have gained the love of
a whole people with such ease."

Louis succeeded to the throne upon the death of his grandfather in
May 1774 and soon showed himself to be a conscientious king, but
not a strong or decisive one. His opinion could be easily swayed by

OPPOSITE
*One of Marie Antoinette's
typically lavish hairstyles,
known as a pouf, c. 1780.
The styles kept growing
taller and heavier until her
hair began to fall out.*

advisors, but he still heeded the advice he'd been given about not letting Marie Antoinette influence him and, even though they had developed a genuine fondness for each other, he stopped her from appointing officials or doing more than dictate the latest fashions and design entertainments at court. Moreover, he and his wife had little in common. Hunting remained his predominant passion, while she enjoyed watching the horse racing in the Bois de Boulogne, gambling on card games such as lansquenet and pharaoh, arranging singing and dancing parties and, on one occasion, organizing a lavish party to see in the dawn in the gardens at Versailles. Louis gave her the Petit Trianon, a small palace attached to Versailles, and she enjoyed choosing the interior decor and planting a *jardin anglais*. By the end of 1776 the queen was running into debt, but the king did not complain. She had struggled with homesickness at first and he was pleased now to see her happy. She had many close friends, both male and female, a vast wardrobe, and a husband who was tender and affectionate in private, if not in public.

One cloud on the horizon was the continued activity of the *libellistes*, who mocked the royal couple relentlessly. When Marie Antoinette got pregnant, rumors spread that Louis was not the father and caricatures showed him with a cuckold's horns. In fact, many biographers suspect she may have had an affair with the very handsome Swedish Count Fersen, who remained a close friend till the end of her life, but it is unlikely that any of her children were his. *Libellistes* wrote of the Dionysian feasts and frivolities at Versailles, and accused her of

BELOW
Marie Antoinette's bedchamber in the Petit Trianon at Versailles. Mirrored panels could be raised to cover the windows, offering the privacy she craved and allowing her to relax and shake off the cares of the court.

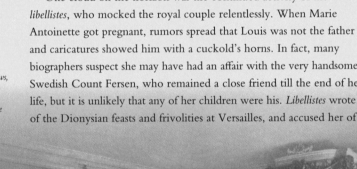

having many lovers, both male and female. Whenever family members visited from Austria, she was said to be siphoning off French money to them, and she was also supposed to be plotting to poison her husband and put one of her lovers on the throne. Then in July 1785 came the so-called Diamond Necklace Affair, an unfortunate plot in which a Cardinal believed that Marie Antoinette wanted him to buy her a necklace of 647 diamonds without her husband finding out. He ordered the necklace, she claimed to know nothing of it, and when the case ended up in court, a con artist named Jeanne de la Motte, the Cardinal's then-mistress, was found guilty of forging letters from the Queen and sentenced to flogging, branding, and life imprisonment. Public opinion, with little respect for the facts, blamed Marie Antoinette, and she was hissed at in the street and called "Madame Déficit" for her profligacy.

She was hissed at in the street and called "Madame Déficit" for her profligacy

ABOVE
In this contemporary cartoon, Louis XVI wears the horns of a cuckold while Marie-Antoinette has a Medusa-style head sporting ostrich feathers.

Louis became depressed at the change in public mood but couldn't decide how to counteract it. Instead, he went hunting more often, ate "immoderate meals," and wept openly in front of his advisors. A poor harvest in 1788, followed by a harsh winter of freezing temperatures meant that bread prices shot up. And then, on July 14, 1789, a mob stormed the Bastille prison in Paris. A hundred were killed, seventy wounded, and only seven prisoners were released, but the events that day and the passions unleashed would soon shake the world.

VIVE LA REVOLUTION!

French citizens were sick and tired of aristocrats enjoying lavish lifestyles while they starved, and a new National Assembly was set up to limit the powers of the monarchy and give more autonomy to the people. When Louis XVI traveled to Paris to try and promote calm, it became clear that he no longer had any authority. On a terrifying night in October 1789, a mob of Parisian market women descended on Versailles demanding grain. They broke into the palace threatening the queen's life, forcing her to escape down a secret

THE EXECUTION OF MONARCHS

Throughout history many reigning monarchs have been executed by foreign invaders, but to be executed by your own subjects must have been a bitter pill indeed. The evening before his own death, Louis XVI took comfort from reading an account of the execution of Charles I of England, who himself had been beheaded in January 1649. Charles had asked his jailer to bring him an extra shirt before walking out to the scaffold, saying, "The season is so sharp as may probably make me shake, which some observers may imagine proceeds from fear. I would have no such imputation." When Maximilian I of Mexico was executed in 1867, he gave his executioners some gold and asked them not to shoot him in the head so that his mother could see his face after death. Nicholas II of Russia was taken by surprise when his family was woken in the middle of the night in July 1918 and led to a basement room. When told he was to be executed he only had time to exclaim, "What? What?" before being riddled with bullets.

RIGHT
The execution of Louis XVI, who was by then known as citizen Louis Capet.

staircase. Many of the nobility fled France at this time, and Marie Antoinette could have returned to Austria but instead chose to stay and help her husband try to restore faith in the monarchy. The National Assembly insisted the family move to the Tuileries Palace in Paris, where they could be more directly supervised and where they were kept under armed guard for the next few years.

In 1791, a new constitution was declared in France under which the monarchy had much less power. With every day that passed, the situation became progressively more perilous for anyone with aristocratic blood, as increasing numbers of the nobility were arrested and charged with crimes against the people. Marie Antoinette's friend Count Fersen devised a plan to rescue the royal family from Paris and help them fight back against the revolutionaries from exile. Louis wavered, so that when they did finally flee, they were easily recaptured at the border. In April 1792 their position went from bad to worse when France declared war on Austria. In September, the monarchy was abolished and the family were told they were ordinary citizens with the surname Capet. And then Louis was arrested and charged with high treason and crimes against the state, as it was now alleged he had colluded with Austria in their invasion of

HELL BROKE LOOSE, OR, THE MURDER OF LOUIS.

France. He defended himself
but was found guilty and
sentenced to execution by a
narrow majority of deputies
in the National Convention.
The sentence was carried out
on January 21, 1793, and Louis
met his death with dignity, even
when prevented from delivering
the speech he had planned to
make on the scaffold.

Marie Antoinette went
into deep mourning on her
husband's death, refusing all
food. By this time she was ill
with diabetes and experiencing
severe hemorrhages, which may
have been a symptom of uterine
cancer. The debate raged about
what to do with her, some
arguing they should return her
to Austria in exchange for
prisoners of war; but in October

MARIE ANTOINETTE

1793, she was finally brought for trial in front of the Revolutionary
Council. The charges included arranging orgies, sending millions
of livres of French money to Austria, and, most ridiculously of all,
committing incest with her own son. To this last accusation she cried,
"Nature itself refuses to respond to such a charge made against a
mother." The verdict was a foregone conclusion; she was found guilty
and taken to the guillotine on October 16, 1793. Among her last
words, she apologized to the executioner on whose toes she had
accidentally trodden as she climbed the scaffold. She was thirty-eight
years old.

Neither Louis nor Marie Antoinette deserved their fate. They were
charitable monarchs who gave generously to the needy, and her
extravagance was not unusual for the time and her position as first
lady. It wasn't a love match and they didn't have much in common,
but they grew to care deeply for each other. Their tragedy was that
she was an easy scapegoat, an enemy alien on whom the French could
blame all their troubles—and he was simply too weak to protect her.

ABOVE
Marie Antoinette at her
trial. She was given less
than a day to prepare her
defense to the charges, most
of which appeared to be
taken straight from satirical
articles written by the
libellistes without any
evidence to support them.

Napoleon Bonaparte
– & –
Joséphine de Beauharnais

Napoleone Buonaparte
Born: August 15, 1769, Corsica
Died: May 5, 1821, Longwood, St. Helena

Joséphine Tascher de la Pagerie
Born: June 23, 1763, Les Trois-Îlets, Martinique
Died: May 29, 1814, Île-de-France, France

Married: March 9, 1796

Joséphine Beauharnais.
Circa 1793.

Joséphine was a sensual, exotic, easy-going, and generous-natured woman

They could not have been more opposite in their characters and backgrounds, but from their first meeting Napoleon was utterly besotted with the glamorous Joséphine, unable to resist her "extraordinary grace" and her "irresistibly sweet manner."

Napoleon and Joséphine were both born on islands: he on the craggy Mediterranean isle of Corsica, which had been conquered by the French in the year of his birth after fierce battles with the nationalist locals; she on the paradise colony of Martinique in the Caribbean, where her family lived in luxury on a sugar plantation. As if the landscapes of their birth somehow determined their characters, he was a blunt, forthright character of strong opinions and iron will, while she was a sensual, exotic, easy-going, and generous-natured woman.

Napoleon's was a close-knit family, with eight children and a domineering, ambitious mother. His father was an assistant judge, affording them a better standard of living than most Corsicans. At the age of nine, Napoleon was sent to France to be educated at a college in Autun, then a military academy in Brienne, before being accepted at the École Militaire in Paris. By sixteen, he was an officer in the French army, joining a regiment at Valence. Napoleon was just nineteen years old when the Bastille prison was stormed in July 1789, and he was all in favor of the Revolution. In his opinion, the King had become too powerful and a new constitution was required to ensure he only acted in the interests of the French people. But the young soldier did not foresee the bloody nature of the forces that had been unleashed, forces that led to the mob violence of September 1792, the execution of King Louis XVI and Queen Marie Antoinette in 1793, and what was known as *Le Terreur*—a period between 1793 and 1794 when tens of thousands were guillotined on the flimsiest of evidence. In August 1794, Napoleon himself was imprisoned for two weeks on a charge of conspiracy, but released when no one could find any grounds to substantiate it.

Joséphine was educated in Martinique, with a curriculum that focused more on music, dancing, and behaving in a ladylike fashion than on intellectual pursuits. When she was fifteen, her aunt wrote from Paris that she was seeking a wife for an aristocratic officer named Alexandre de Beauharnais, the younger son of her lover. Joséphine was eager to go, and delighted when she arrived in France and met the dashing Alexandre. They were married in December 1779, but it wasn't long before they were disappointed in each other. He was irritated by her lack of cultural education and poor literacy skills, while she was distressed by his constant philandering. They had two children, Eugène and Hortense, but by 1782 the marriage was over in all but name. During the early years of the Revolution, Alexandre became President of the Constituent Assembly but had fallen out of favor by the spring of 1794 and was thrown into jail. As his wife, Joséphine was also arrested and imprisoned in an old Carmelite monastery. In July that year, during *Le Terreur*, Alexandre was executed. Joséphine was terrified that she would meet the same fate,

BELOW
Napoleon I reviewing his cavalry troops behind the Arc de Triomphe, a monument he commissioned in 1806 shortly after his victory over a Russo-Austrian army at the Battle of Austerlitz. The Arc was designed to commemorate all those who had died for their country in the Revolutionary and Napoleonic Wars of the previous seventeen years.

but in August 1794 she was unexpectedly released
and reunited with her children as the period
of bloodletting came to an end.

Napoleon was sickened by the violence of
Le Terreur and wrote a pamphlet urging French
citizens to avoid all-out civil war. In October
1795, he helped to crush a revolt in Paris
against the new constitution and as his
reward was appointed Commander-in-Chief
of the Army of the Interior. An order was
issued that all unauthorized weapons held
by private citizens had to be handed in to
the authorities. Joséphine's fourteen-year-old
son, Eugène, wanted to keep the sword that had
belonged to his father and went to ask permission
of General Bonaparte. Napoleon agreed to his
request, and the following day Joséphine came in
person to thank the general for his kindness. She was so warm
and friendly at this first meeting that Napoleon asked if he might call
on her some time. She invited him to one of the regular Thursday
receptions she held and he wasted no time in taking up the offer.

ABOVE
*Napoleon claimed that
Joséphine "possessed an
exact knowledge of all the
intricacies of [his] character,
and with it an admirable
tact." She knew how to
soothe his bad moods
and ease the load of his
heavy responsibilities.*

A PASSIONATE, ALL-CONSUMING LOVE

At twenty-six years old, Napoleon was shy and awkward around
women. There had been a couple of dalliances, but his only sexual
experience had been with prostitutes. Joséphine, on the other hand,
had taken a few lovers since the breakup of her marriage and at
thirty-two was very much a woman of the world. She had a slender
figure, masses of curly chestnut hair, and she dressed fashionably
in the Neoclassical style, with soft, flowing dresses, plunging
necklines, and bare arms. Gracious and hospitable, she was an
excellent conversationalist and a natural flirt. Before long, she had
invited Napoleon to her bed, and he fell passionately, obsessively,
in love with her. "I awaken full of you," he wrote. "Between your
portrait and the memory of our intoxicating night, my senses have
no respite." He bombarded her with love letters and proposals of
marriage and in March 1796, less than five months after they first
met, she became his wife in a civil ceremony.

Two days later, Napoleon left to command the army in Italy, but
he continued to write to Joséphine twice daily with unrelenting ardor.

"Every day since I met you I have loved you a thousand times more," he wrote, and was upset by the casual tone of her replies and the long gaps between her letters. He repeatedly begged her to join him in the south, but she was reluctant to leave Paris because, unknown to Napoleon, she was ensconced in an affair with a young man called Hippolyte Charles. While her husband won glorious victories against the Austrians, driving them back to their own soil, she dallied with Hippolyte and only traveled to join the heroic commander of the French army at the end of June. Her affair continued for two years during which Napoleon heard sporadic rumors of it until eventually presented with proof while he was fighting at the head of the army in Egypt in 1798. According to his secretary, "a wild look came into his eyes, and several times he struck his head with his fists." His heart was completely broken. He had a brief affair himself, as a kind of revenge, but when he returned to Paris to confront Joséphine, she won her way back into his affections with a mixture of tears and seduction. She was still his Joséphine, but from then on the dynamic of the marriage had changed. Before, he had been the pursuer, the one who was most in love; now she realized how much she needed him and took it upon herself to be his loving, supportive partner, the one who could make him relax at the end of a long day.

The days were stressful indeed in the autumn of 1799, as Napoleon planned the coup d'état that would rid the country of the corrupt, discredited post-revolutionary government and bring him to power. Through a combination of political

BELOW
Napoleon the Great. At its largest his Empire encompassed some seventy million people across Europe, and he oversaw every aspect of its control.

> "*Every day since I met you I have loved you a thousand times more*"

NAPOLEON LE GRAND

gamesmanship and threats, he established himself as First Consul of France with Joséphine as his first lady. She was adept at hosting receptions for ambassadors and other dignitaries, always knowing exactly the right thing to say. She also became skilled at reading Napoleon's mood and learning when he needed diversion. He loved spending time in her boudoir, watching as she had her hair styled or her face painted. The only thing they ever fought about was her debts; she spent vast sums of money on clothes and shoes, as well as flowers for the gardens of Malmaison, a château she was renovating as a retreat for them both.

Napoleon was a shrewd, decisive leader, whom the French people trusted, and in a plebiscite in the spring of 1802, he was elected First Consul for life. In 1804, no one batted an eyelid when he became Emperor of the French Republic with the right to choose his successor—even though the Revolution had been fought precisely to overthrow the principle of hereditary power. And therein lay a problem for Napoleon, because Joséphine, now in her late thirties, had not managed to provide him with an heir.

THE FLOWERS OF MALMAISON

In 1799, while Napoleon was fighting the Egyptian campaign, Joséphine bought an estate seven miles west of Paris that enclosed nearly 150 acres of land. Her plan was to turn it into "the most beautiful and curious garden in Europe," with rare plants from around the world but especially from her native Martinique. She was assisted in the English-style design of the park by Louis-Martin Berthault, a prominent landscape architect. Among her ambitious schemes, she grew pineapples in a heated orangery, and a rose garden with 250 different varieties of roses. By the time of her death, she had established 200 new plants that had never been grown in France before. She also kept exotic animals in the grounds, including kangaroos, gazelles, ostriches, and zebras. Although Napoleon balked at the cost of the estate, he found it a peaceful and lovely spot. In 1815, during his return from exile on Elba, he visited Malmaison and sat with Joséphine's daughter Hortense in the garden, talking of Joséphine. "Wouldn't it be delightful if we could remain here forever," he sighed wistfully.

LEFT
The Emperor and Empress relaxing in the sumptuous gardens at Malmaison.

A MAN NEEDS A SON

On the evening of the December 1, 1804, Napoleon and Joséphine were wed in a religious ceremony. The following day was their coronation, at which, despite the presence of the Pope, Napoleon took the imperial crown and placed it on his own head before crowning his wife. According to witnesses, "She knelt down with such simple elegance that all eyes were delighted with the picture she presented." Surely her position must now be unassailable, even without an heir?

Joséphine had tried over the years to get pregnant, taking many spa cures, but to no avail. She arranged the marriage of her daughter Hortense to Napoleon's younger brother Louis and, after they had a son, suggested to her husband that he might adopt the boy and train him as a successor. However, Napoleon's sisters had been opposed to Joséphine from the start and they schemed behind the scenes to persuade him to cast her aside and take a younger wife. His sister Caroline introduced him to an eighteen-year-old beauty named Eléonore Denuelle de la Plaigne, who got pregnant after a brief affair with him in September 1806, thus apparently proving that it was Joséphine who was infertile and not him. Napoleon arranged Eléonore's marriage to one of her lieutenants and gave her a large dowry, but had nothing to do with the boy. All the same, Joséphine was naturally upset by this, and found it even more painful to say

BELOW
Napoleon crowns his wife in Notre Dame, in the presence of Pope Pius VII. By taking the crowns in his own hands instead of letting the Pope crown them, Napoleon was signaling that, as Emperor, his authority transcended that of any religion.

farewell to her husband as he rode northeast shortly
afterwards to fight a coalition of Russian and Prussian
forces. She worried about the separation, and was not
surprised to hear that he had taken a Polish mistress,
Marie Walewska. When she wrote to Napoleon
asking if she might come and join him, he put her
off with excuses about the difficulty of the journey.
It was ten months before they would see each other
again. She didn't know it but the Emperor had
already decided to divorce her and had drawn up
a list of potential marriage candidates, most of them
less than half Joséphine's age.

In November 1809, when Napoleon finally told
his wife he was divorcing her, she collapsed with
grief. The terms he offered were generous: she
retained the rank of "crowned and appointed empress" and the title
"Your Majesty." She had the château at Malmaison and the use of
the Elysée Palace in Paris, as well as an allowance of three million
francs a year, and all her debts were paid off. At the formal signing of
the separation agreement, Napoleon read out a statement that began,
"Only God knows what this resolve has cost my heart." It was clear
he still loved her but was only divorcing her because she had failed to
give him an heir. Joséphine's statement read, "I proudly offer him the
greatest proof of attachment and devotion ever given a husband on
this earth." They kissed and Joséphine broke down in tears. For some
weeks after the divorce, they continued to see each other regularly,
until the end of March 1810, when Napoleon's new bride-to-be,
eighteen-year-old Archduchess Marie Louise of Austria, was due
to arrive. At that point, Napoleon gave Joséphine the Château de
Navarre in Normandy and asked her to stay there, well out of the
way, while Marie Louise settled in to her new role—the role that
had once been Joséphine's.

ABOVE
*Marie Louise of Austria
was not a great beauty
but she knew her role
and acquiesced without
a murmur in anything
Napoleon asked her to do.*

AN HEIR, AN EXILE, AND AN END

On March 20, 1811, the Empress Marie Louise fulfilled her part
of the bargain and gave birth to a son, whom Napoleon planned to
make his successor as Emperor of the French. By then the empire
stretched over almost the whole of Western Europe—from Portugal
to the North Sea and from the toe of Italy to the Russian border—
as well as to farther-flung colonies, encompassing a population of 70

NAPOLEON'S LEGACY

Napoleon brought stability to France as it emerged from the most shockingly violent period in its recent history. Among the reforms he instituted was the Napoleonic Code, a set of laws that allowed freedom of religion and forbade any privileges based on birth, decreeing instead that government jobs should go to those best qualified for them. It was a hugely important document, which influenced several other legal systems around the world and spurred nationalist revolt in a number of countries. He commissioned many imposing new buildings in Paris, including the Arc de Triomphe, a new wing for the Louvre Museum, and the Vendôme column. Throughout the country he modernized the transport infrastructure, building new roads, harbors, and canals, and ordered that the roads be lined with poplar trees—a legacy that can still be seen in France today. His military theories influenced armies across Europe and America and some military historians still consider him the greatest commander of all time.

RIGHT
Napoleon in Fontainebleau on March 31, 1814, after Paris had been captured. Two days later he was deposed as Emperor.

million people in all. Napoleon's military genius made him a formidable foe, but in 1812 he overstretched himself and set in motion the forces that would lead to his downfall when he marched his army into Russia. As he advanced on Moscow, the Russians retreated, burning crops along the way, so there was no food for Napoleon's army. By December 5, with the men starving and winter closing in fast, Napoleon decided that he must head back to France, leaving his soldiers to struggle home on their own. Of 600,000 men who went with him to Russia, only a tenth survived.

In spring 1813, his support crumbling, Napoleon had to fight British forces under the Duke of Wellington in Spain as well as a new Russian–Prussian alliance in Germany. The challenge was insurmountable, even for him, and on April 6, 1814, he accepted the inevitable and abdicated as Emperor. Marie Louise escaped back to Austria with their son

and Napoleon was told he would be exiled to the island of Elba off the coast of Italy. Marie Louise brought up their son in Austria, where he died of tuberculosis in 1832 without ever ruling France as his father had wished.

Napoleon wrote one last letter to Joséphine, saying "Never forget him who has never forgotten, and never will forget, you." She told her lady-in-waiting, "It is, above all, at this moment when he has been forgotten and abandoned that I would wish to help him bear his exile and share his grief." But she felt she could not join him in Elba now that he was married to another, and then fate stepped in to make it impossible. In early May 1814 Joséphine caught a chill while out driving in a flimsy gown. She rallied but was forced to take to her bed after the illness worsened. On May 29, with her son and daughter by her bedside, she passed away, probably from diphtheria. According to her son, she went "as sweetly and gently to meet death as she had met life."

When the news reached Elba, Napoleon was inconsolable. She had been his lucky charm and without her by his side, his fortunes had declined. He wasn't ready to give up on power, though, and in March 1815, nine months after Joséphine's death, he landed in the south of France and made his way back to Paris to reclaim the crown from Louis XVIII, brother of Louis XVI, the king who had been executed during the French Revolution. His comeback lasted just a hundred days before he was again defeated, at the Battle of Waterloo, and this time he was exiled to the remote island of St. Helena in the middle of the South Atlantic Ocean. There, as he worked on his memoirs, his thoughts often dwelled on Joséphine. "She was a woman to her utter fingertips," he wrote. "Elegant, charming and affable . . . and she was so kind, so humane—she was the best woman in France." According to one of his companions, the Count de Montholon, when Napoleon died in 1821, at the age of fifty-two, his last mumbled words were, "France, the Army, Head of the Army, Joséphine."

> "*She was a woman to her utter fingertips . . . elegant, charming and affable . . . she was the best woman in France*"

ABOVE
During his final illness, Napoleon became convinced that Joséphine was by his bedside and according to his companion, the Count de Montholon, he said, "She told me we were going to see each other again and never again leave each other."

Ludwig I of Bavaria
– & –
Lola Montez

Ludwig I
Born: August 25, 1786, Strasbourg, France
Died: February 29, 1868, Nice, France

Elizabeth Rosanna Gilbert
Born: February 17, 1821, Sligo, Ireland
Died: January 17, 1861, New York City

ABOVE
*Ludwig was hard of hearing and had a persistent stammer,
but neither of these disabilities stopped him from pursuing
any pretty woman who crossed his path.*

Ludwig commissioned fine neoclassical buildings, amassed an impressive collection of art and sculpture, built canals and railways, and managed to juggle the demands of neighboring countries and opposing religious groups. He wasn't a bad monarch for his day —until he completely lost his head on meeting controversial courtesan Lola Montez.

When Ludwig was born in the French city of Strasbourg, his father, an officer in the French army, was third in line for the position of Elector of Bavaria. There were Electors of each of the states of the Holy Roman Empire, the role being equivalent to that of a prince, but there seemed no real prospect that Ludwig would ever be a king. He was christened the day after his birth, with Marie-Antoinette, Queen of France, agreeing to be the boy's godmother. The French King, Louis XVI, gave him diamonds as a christening present, while the men in his father's regiment shaved off their beards to stuff a pillow for him.

In 1789, when Ludwig was just three years old, the French Revolution began. By 1792 the monarchy had been overthrown, Ludwig's godmother was guillotined just months after the King's execution, and Ludwig's family fled to safety across the border into Germany. There he was educated by tutors before studying at the universities in Landshut and Göttingen. All the while, the line of succession was getting shorter— after his uncle's death in 1795, his father became Duke of Zweibrücken; in 1799, after the death of the Elector of Bavaria, his father assumed that role as well; and in 1806 he became King Maximilian, with Ludwig a prince.

Young Prince Ludwig traveled extensively in Italy and Greece and developed a taste for Greek architecture and Italian art, as well as for women—lots of women. He wasn't a good-looking man, with soft features and a complexion marked by smallpox scars, but his regal status helped him to make conquests. In 1810, he married Princess Therese of Saxe-Hildburghausen, said to

BELOW
Princess Therese of Saxe-Hildburghausen, Ludwig's wife: she was very popular with Bavarian citizens, who saw her as the ideal wife and mother and praised her for her charitable work.

LUDWIG'S WOMEN

Marianna Marchesa Florenzi, an Italian noblewoman, was Ludwig's lover and close friend for more than 40 years and they corresponded on affairs of state as well as affairs of the heart. More than 3,000 of her letters survive, along with 1,500 of his. English society beauty Jane Digby was his mistress in the early 1830s and married a Bavarian baron as a cover for their passionate affair. Ludwig romanced actresses and dancers as well as aristocratic ladies and, in his later years, had a crush on one of his daughter's ladies-in-waiting. All were immortalized in Ludwig's "Gallery of Beauties," a collection of thirty-six portraits painted between 1827 and 1850 of the women he considered most lovely. It included the actress Charlotte von Hagn, shoemaker's daughter Helene Sedlmayer, members of the Bavarian nobility—and many of the king's mistresses, including the most famous of them all, Lola Montez.

RIGHT
Ludwig was generally considered a good king before his affair with Lola Montez.

be the best-looking princess in Europe at the time, a match that was extremely popular with the people of Bavaria, not least because she was Protestant. The country had a population that was two-thirds Catholic and a third Protestant, and since he was Catholic, his choice of bride was politically expedient. She would be a good wife, producing eight children for him and turning a blind eye to his affairs with other women, a habit he had taken up again even in the early days of the marriage.

Ludwig did not agree with his father's policy of appeasing Napoleon Bonaparte, the expansionist ruler of France, but after the defeat of Austria and Russia he had no choice but to fight in the Napoleonic Wars on the French side, commanding the 1st Bavarian Division. The Confederation of the Rhine was a union of sixteen German states, all backing Napoleon on the eastern front. It was only in 1813 that the Confederation was dissolved and Bavaria was able to change allegiance and declare war on her neighbor. At the Congress of Vienna in 1815, when the map of Europe was being redrawn after Napoleon's defeat, Ludwig spoke out in favor of the unification of the German states, feeling that there would be strength in unity; it was a goal he would continue to hold, although one he personally would never achieve.

In 1825, his father died and Ludwig became King of Bavaria. He was a benign ruler at first, carefully balancing the political power of different religious groups in the government. There was a strong faction of

ABOVE
*In March 1848, King
Frederick William IV of
Prussia promised that the
state would be merged into
a united Germany, but was
too late to stop his citizens
rebelling against the police
force and storming the
arsenal in Berlin. He kept
his throne but lost most of
his powers.*

ultramontane Jesuits who wanted the Pope to have more authority
in running the country, to the alarm of the Protestant minority.
There was also growing unrest about the strict censorship in the
country, this being opposed by university students in particular,
while an even wider number of citizens opposed the high levels of
taxation. Ludwig focused his energy on industrializing the country,
linking the rivers Main and Danube with a canal and building the
country's first railway line between Nuremberg and Fürth to allow
for easier transportation of goods. He built the Valhalla, a replica of
the Parthenon on the banks of the Danube, and commissioned the
Ludwigstrasse boulevard in Munich as well as art galleries and classical
monuments, and he collected art from Italy, Germany, and Holland.
In the royal household he was notoriously frugal, and dressed
eccentrically in ill-fitting coats, often strolling the streets of Munich
rather than traveling in carriages.

There were rumblings of revolution around Europe in the early
1840s, but Ludwig largely ignored them. When there were riots
in 1844 after he introduced a tax on beer, he quickly decreed a
10 percent reduction in the price. Perhaps he would have survived
the revolutions that swept Europe in 1848; it seems likely that he
could have remained on the throne, were it not for one woman:
Lola Montez.

A LOOSE CANNON

Lola Montez was a born liar. She lied about her name, her age, her birthplace and nationality, her parentage, her marital status, and her lovers. She most often claimed to be Spanish, but in fact she was probably born in Sligo, Ireland, to an illegitimate mother and an army officer father. The family sailed to India in March 1823, but within days of their arrival her father had died of cholera and her mother married his friend, Captain Patrick Craigie, who took on the role of stepfather to the young Lola. She was a beautiful, dark-haired creature, but wild, short-tempered, and mischievous; among her exploits, she enjoyed pushing unsuspecting villagers into a snake-infested creek. Her mother decided she was too much of a handful and in 1826 sent her back to be educated in Scotland, but Lola caused trouble wherever she went, it seemed, and was moved

RIGHT
Lola Montez was lovely to behold, and it was said that "no one could withstand the charm of [her] smile at close range," though "her wit was that of the pot-house [tavern]."

around several different schools. In 1836, when Lola was fifteen, her mother sailed to England hoping to marry Lola to a rich older man. Instead, to her mother's exasperation, Lola began a flirtation with a young lieutenant called Thomas James, who became her first lover and, before long, her first husband. They married in July 1837 and set sail for India together, but Lola was soon bored of him, saying "A long trip suffocates love." By 1840 her marriage was over and she was on her way back to London. From then on, she would have to resort to a variety of methods of earning a living that no decent lady of the time would have contemplated.

> *"Lola's beauty, particularly the splendor of her breasts, made madmen everywhere"*

There was always a string of male protectors who were happy to pay Lola's bills in return for her favors. "Lola's beauty, particularly the splendor of her breasts, made madmen everywhere," wrote her German biographer Edward Fuchs. She took an acting course and launched herself on the London stage as "Spanish Dancer, Donna Maria Dolores de Porris y Montez." The reviews were mixed, praising her beauty rather than her talent, but when some journalists began to question her invented Spanish background, she decided it was time to move on. Lola decamped to mainland Europe, where in Dresden she had a brief affair with composer and piano virtuoso Franz Liszt—she may also have been the lover of Alexandre Dumas Sr. in Paris—before arriving in Munich on October 5, 1846.

Three days later she had a private meeting with Ludwig I to request his permission to dance on the stage of the Hoftheater. One report of this encounter relates that the King admired her bosom and asked if it was real, whereupon she produced a pair of scissors and cut away the fabric of her dress to display it to him in full. This may or may not be true, but whatever happened, the King was captivated by her from that moment. He asked if she would sit for a portrait that he could display in his famous Gallery of Beauties, and she consented. Within a month of her arrival, he had awarded her an annual allowance of 10,000 florins. (By comparison, a university professor might have expected to earn 2,000 florins a year at that time.) Within two months, he had bought her a house and provided further funds for her to decorate and furnish it. All this was before he had enjoyed any sexual favors at all; she kept him dangling as she attempted to launch herself into Bavarian society.

LOLA MONTEZ.
COUNTESS OF LANDSFELD.

ABOVE
In just seventeen months, Lola turned the vast majority of the Bavarian people against her and was instrumental in destroying both Ludwig and his kingdom.

OPPOSITE
As revolution broke out, Ludwig persuaded Lola to retire to Lake Constance, near the Swiss border, while he tried to appease his people. But it wasn't far enough, and soon they were together again. "The world isn't capable of making me break with you," he wrote.

Many people warned Ludwig against Lola. His chief of police discovered that before arriving in Munich she had been expelled from Baden-Baden, Berlin, and Warsaw for lewd, disruptive behavior. Some told Ludwig that Lola had other lovers and that she bragged of her political influence over him. A few suspected she was a spy planted in their midst by the British Prime Minister, Lord Palmerston, in hopes of inciting revolution. The Bavarian people were horrified by the lack of respect she showed to their King, refusing to stand when he arrived at the theatre and addressing him familiarly before she had first been spoken to. But Ludwig defended her against all charges as he fell deeper and deeper in love. " Her friendship has made me purer, better," he insisted, despite all evidence to the contrary. If he questioned Lola about any alleged misdemeanors (such as attacking an official in the post office), she reacted with such fury that he backed down immediately. She had a short fuse and frequently resorted to physical violence if she didn't get her own way.

Now there was a new demand: Lola wanted Ludwig to make her a countess, for which she would first have to become a naturalized citizen of Bavaria. The besotted king set the wheels in motion. Anyone who had a word to say against Lola found his or her career in ruins. Those who refused to tip their hat to her in the street found themselves in jail. She began to influence Ludwig's policy-making, swaying him toward liberalism and influencing him against conservatives and Jesuits. By early 1847, Lola had offended people at all levels of Bavarian society. The head of the Kunstverein (arts club) wrote: "The nobility is disgusted, the burghers are angry, and even the protestant party, who hope to profit by the present state of things, agree that the King of Bavaria has 'lost his senses'." The Minister of the Interior, Karl August von Abel, resigned, saying "Bavaria believes itself ruled by a foreigner whom the public regards as a branded woman." The British Foreign Office wrote of "a signal degradation of Royal dignity." But still Ludwig defended his feisty mistress against all criticism.

A KING IS DETHRONED

In June 1847, Lola's grip over the King tightened during a "honeymoon" they spent together at Bad Brückenau. He had a foot fetish and she allowed him to suck her pretty toes, giving him pieces of her undergarments to wear next to his skin. On his birthday in August, Ludwig fulfilled his promise by making her the Countess of Landsfeld and Lola was over the moon. At last, she thought, society would have to show her the respect she craved—but it was not to be. Queen Therese still refused to receive her and the aristocracy followed suit, leaving her visiting cards unanswered, much to her fury.

In the second half of 1847, Lola became friends with some men from the scandalous Allemania student fraternity, known for their raucous parties and bad behavior—in which Lola was happy to indulge. Crowds of citizens began to protest openly against her, surrounding her house and demanding her expulsion from Bavaria. At Lola's urging, Ludwig responded by closing the universities, where rebellion was being fomented. There were further resignations and the rector of the university handed Ludwig a list of Lola's felonies, insisting on her immediate departure.

In January and February of 1848, revolutions were spreading across Europe as the working classes demanded better living conditions and the middle classes demanded freedom from strict state control; Italy and France were first, followed by rebellions in the German states. Ludwig was in a precarious

CONTRACEPTION IN THE 19TH CENTURY

Courtesans like Lola had many methods at their disposal to prevent inconvenient, unwanted pregnancies. Condoms could be purchased, made from skin taken from the bladder or intestine of an animal and treated with chemicals—but these were expensive, certainly far too pricey for an ordinary prostitute. Linen condoms, used in the previous century by Casanova, had gone out of fashion. Many women drank traditional herbal infusions containing saxifrage, rue, pennyroyal, sage, and feverfew to prevent pregnancy. A London tailor and social reformer called Francis Place developed a contraceptive sponge that was designed not to decrease pleasure. It was the size of "a green walnut or small apple" and was attached to a double thread for easy removal. It is not documented which method of contraception Lola used, but she is not thought ever to have got pregnant. It is said she suffered from syphilis, which she passed on to Ludwig, from which we can assume that she was not using barrier methods.

position and Lola had to go—but not too far. He sent her to Lindau on the shore of Lake Constance, near the border with Switzerland. She wrote to him proclaiming histrionically that her heart was broken; as always he gave in and replied that he would meet her in Lausanne just as soon as he could slip away. But that wasn't good enough for Lola; she sneaked back to Munich disguised as a man and had a three-hour meeting with the King. He wrote to her straight afterward, still besotted, "I picked out your vest to put on and in the presence of my servants couldn't resist giving it a kiss." It was behavior like this that would seal his fate. News of the meeting leaked out and any remaining support for Ludwig crumbled. On March 20, 1848, he was forced to abdicate his throne. It wasn't entirely Lola's fault, but she was the single most important factor counting against him.

AN ITINERANT LIFE

After his abdication, Ludwig returned to Bavaria, but following his wife Therese's death in 1854 he spent increasing amounts of time in Italy. Ludwig and Lola never saw each other again, but they continued to correspond and he was unable to refuse whenever she wrote to him demanding money. He learned that Lola had been sleeping with several

BELOW
An American audience member laughs out loud at Lola's amateurish dancing while another looks horrified behind his newspaper. But she was irrepressible; when she got into trouble, she simply moved on and reinvented herself in a new location.

other men while in Munich and wrote to her, "Your infidelities have deceived my heart but still it forgives you." In 1849, Ludwig turned for comfort to the Catholic religion and urged Lola to do the same.

However, Lola spent the 1850s living as scandalously as she had in the previous decade. She married a man named George Trafford Heald for his money and was then arrested and charged with bigamy (the divorce from James had not been entirely legal), forcing her to flee across the Atlantic. She invented a Spider Dance, which she premiered on the New York stage in December 1849. In it, she played two characters: a spider spinning a web, then a young girl caught up in the web. She married for a third time and toured America with her show, taking a horsewhip to more than one journalist who wrote a scathing review. In 1855, she undertook a tour of Australia, and three years later published her autobiography, denying that she had ever been a mistress of Ludwig I and relating how she had been "saved and brought to Jesus." She died in New York after a stroke and colorful obituaries ran in papers around the globe. "Plenty of animal spirits, pluck, talked well, and could dance a little," wrote the *New York Herald*.

> "*Your infidelities have deceived my heart but still it forgives you*"

ABOVE
Ludwig I in 1860, the year before Lola's death. He continued his involvement in cultural projects after his abdication, but never again saw his lively one-time mistress.

It took Ludwig a long time to recover from his infatuation. He kept sending her money until 1851 even though he knew that by then she was married. "Do you hear anything of Lola Montez?" he wrote to a friend in 1853, despite the fact that she had tried to blackmail him, threatening to print his letters to her. And when a friend of Lola's wrote to tell him of her death in 1861, he replied, "It is a great consolation to hear her deying [sic] as a cristian [sic]. LM was a much distinguished lady." There was no sign of bitterness over the fact that she probably cost him his throne, and that in return he enjoyed fewer of her sexual favors than dozens of her other admirers. She was a larger-than-life character who had held him in such thrall for so many years that he would never be able to think ill of her.

King of Italy &
Countess of Mirafiori & Fontanafredda

Victor Emmanuel II
– & –
Rosa Vercellana

Vittorio Emanuele Maria Alberto Eugenio Ferdinando Tommaso
Born: March 14, 1820, Turin, Italy
Died: January 9, 1878, Rome, Italy

Rosa Vercellana
Born: June 3, 1833, Nice, France
Died: December 26, 1885, Pisa, Italy

Married October 18, 1869

He was a married 27-year-old prince with five children, while the girl was a 13-year-old peasant, but he couldn't resist stopping to talk to her

Victor Emmanuel had been out hunting wild boar in 1847 when
he noticed a girl at the roadside who looked like "a true, fresh,
perfumed rose." He was a married 27-year-old prince with five
children, while the girl was a 13-year-old peasant, but he couldn't
resist stopping to talk to her. From then on he was captivated
and couldn't resist seeking her out again . . .

*Y*oung Victor Emmanuel was born with the weight of history
on his shoulders. Italy was a land divided into eight states,
each with a different ruler, and his father was King of the
state of Piedmont and Sardinia while his mother was an Austrian
archduchess and Princess of the state of Tuscany. Victor grew up aware
of the pressing political problems of the era: Austrian rule of the Italian
states of Lombardy and Venetia, as well as their influence in other
regions of the peninsula, was increasingly unpopular; the reactionary
Catholic Church held much of central Italy in its rigid grip; and
meanwhile the "Young Italy" movement was advocating
a unified Italy made up of democratic states. Across
Europe, the tide had turned against autocratic
rulers and Italy had some catching up to do.

Victor was educated in Piedmont and in
the Renaissance city of Florence, and by
all accounts was a good-humored boy
who enjoyed sports, especially hunting,
and is said to have ridden as well as
any Cossack of the Russian steppes.
From an early age, he took an interest
in political and military matters. He
knew his eventual marriage would be a
matter of political allegiances and did
not object when he was matched with
his cousin Adelaide of Austria, daughter
of the Viceroy of Lombardy and Venetia,
in 1842, but the marriage was frowned upon
by many citizens, who thought it increased
Austrian influence in Italy. Adelaide was a small,

OPPOSITE
*An equestrian statue of
Victor Emmanuel II at
his national monument
in the heart of Rome. The
grandiose white marble
structure is one of the city's
most notable landmarks.*

BELOW
*Adelaide of Austria was
a pious woman who
accepted without question
her arranged marriage to a
first cousin, not to mention
his subsequent affairs.*

pretty woman, a devout Catholic who did a lot of work for charity when she wasn't busy bearing children. On marrying a king, it was the wife's duty to provide an heir, but Adelaide went above and beyond, bearing a child a year during the first five years of their marriage, which must have kept her preoccupied for a time. Meanwhile, it was commonplace for kings to have affairs, and Victor took several mistresses.

There are various romantic versions of Victor's first meeting with Rosa Vercellana, but all are agreed that he had been hunting in the vicinity of Moncalvo in Piedmont when he saw a young girl making garlands of wildflowers by a roadside. He ordered his carriage driver to pull over and climbed down to greet the girl. He was bearded, scruffy and wearing a hunting cap. Rosa's first impression was that he looked like an ogre. He asked her name and she told him. "Will you come for a ride with me?" he asked, pointing to his carriage, and she shook her head, her cheeks flushed. At that, he told her that the following day he would send a carriage lined with silk and pulled by white horses to collect her, and he climbed into his coach and left. In his diary, he wrote about the girl's fresh, stunning appearance as "a miracle of the earth" and he simply couldn't get her out of his mind. She was very young but of marriageable age in mid-19th-century Italy, and she must have been struck by the fairy-tale nature of their meeting long before she learned that her admirer was a genuine prince.

> *He wrote about the girl's fresh, stunning appearance as "a miracle of the earth"*

THE VERCELLANA FAMILY

Rosa's father, Giovanni Battista Vercellana, was a tall, strong Piedmontese man who had been a standard bearer for the French army in the Napoleonic wars and was decorated by Napoleon on the battlefield during the 1815 campaign when he sought to regain the crown of France. Thereafter, Giovanni became an officer in the King's Guard, and by 1847 he was working on the royal hunting estate of Racconigi. He had three children, Dominic, Rosa, and Adelaide, and made extra money for his family by running a stagecoach between Moncalvo, Asti, and Casale.

The day Rosa first met Victor, she was waiting by the roadside for her father to collect her, and when Giovanni finally arrived he was bemused by her tale of an "ogre" who was planning to send a

silk-lined carriage for her. However, the
next evening when Rosa didn't come
home he grew alarmed. She returned
the following day with a garbled
story. The carriage had drawn up
and whisked her off to a castle
where she had been given a
beautiful white satin ball gown
to wear and ate dinner at a long
table, with servants dishing out
sumptuous food. She had slept
in a huge bed, surrounded
by ornate decor, and then she
was brought home again in the
silk-lined carriage. Her father asked
what the man looked like and Rosa
described his long moustache that
curled upward over his cheeks and his
little pointy beard, then mentioned a
coat-of-arms worn on his chest. Giovanni
asked around in the town of Moncalvo and soon
realized it must have been Prince Victor Emmanuel who had
entertained his daughter.

ABOVE
*Victor Emmanuel was a
generous man who was
said never to refuse a favor.
After Italian unification, he
was known as the "Father
of the Fatherland."*

Victor had a good reputation in the area and was known for his
many acts of kindness to his subjects. He often drank coffee in a
coffeehouse in Moncalvo, where he enjoyed debating with friends.
There Victor heard the story of a man from Ottiglio who'd had
a twelfth child and because of a local superstition about twelfth
children, the church refused to baptize him. Victor forced them to
change their minds when he said he would personally stand godfather
to the child, asking that the infant be named after him. Giovanni
hoped that the prince would look after his daughter and was reassured
when he came to visit their humble home, telling them that he
would like to take Rosa under his wing. He wanted to educate her,
to give her a house, nice clothes, a maid, and a hairdresser to tend her
beautiful hair. What would any poor man say? Of course he agreed.

Giovanni must have known what the prince saw in his daughter.
She was a legendary beauty with expressive eyes, thick dark lashes,
glossy jet-black hair, clear white skin, and long elegant hands. Her
figure was tall and well-developed for her age. And there was her

lively intelligence. She had no guile and responded to the world with a natural charm and curiosity that enchanted anyone who met her. With these gifts, it seemed she had won the heart of a prince.

Giovanni trusted that Victor would look after her, and so he did. He gave her a villa near his castle as well as an apartment in Turin and one in the royal estate of Pollenza, so she could always be nearby wherever duty called him. He showered her with gifts of clothes and jewels, and he looked after her family as well, getting a good job for her brother Dominic and even helping her cousins. In return, Rosa became his mistress and the person with whom he could relax when affairs of state were stressful. In December 1848, two years after meeting Victor, she gave birth to a daughter, Vittoria, and three years later she bore him a son, Emanuele. Victor was as delighted with these children as he was with his legitimate children by Princess Adelaide, and told Rosa they were "splendid creations."

But news of the affair was soon common knowledge and the politicians and nobility of Italy were not at all pleased. Victor's father, Charles Albert, warned him of the necessity of avoiding scandal, but he refused to give up his beloved Rosa. And then in 1849, his father abdicated after a humiliating defeat by the Austrian army at the Battle of Novara, and Victor Emmanuel became King of Piedmont-Sardinia, with some very complex political problems on his plate. An affair with a peasant girl was a complication many thought he could do without.

JEALOUSY & BACKBITING

Piedmontese noble ladies were incensed that their king's heart had been stolen by someone so lowly, but Rosa was popular amongst the people of Italy, to whom she was known as "La Bela Rosin" or "Bella Rosina." She didn't put on airs and graces, but every Friday she dressed in black and slipped out to distribute alms and do charitable work, and she was always generous to her friends and family. Victor's wife, Adelaide, knew of the royal mistress but didn't see Rosa as a threat to her position in the way that a noble lady might have been; she didn't often socialize at court, and her taste for flashy jewelry and flamboyant clothes merely underlined her lack of breeding. Then in 1855, Queen Adelaide died while giving birth to her eighth child, and suddenly there was an empty space beside Victor on the throne.

In 1852, Victor had appointed Count Camillo Benso of Cavour as prime minister in what proved to be a shrewd move. Cavour became the mastermind behind the campaign for Italian unification and Victor

OPPOSITE
Rosa and Victor, c. 1860, when he was forty and she was twenty-seven. She was still beautiful, with glossy black hair and dark eyes, while he maintained his elaborate upswept mustache.

"*You have forced me to make it clear to you that Rosina and I will love each other forever*"

CAVOUR & GARIBALDI

The architects of Italian unification were both brilliant men in their own ways, but they hated each other. Prime Minister Cavour was an aristocrat, who used canny deals with friends overseas to help build a strong state in northern Italy and drive the Austrians out. General Giuseppe Garibaldi, on the other hand, was a military man, who distrusted Cavour's behind-the-scenes skulduggery. He thought Italy should be united by means of a democratic uprising, so in 1860 he led his band of Red Shirts on a march (the "Expedition of the Thousand") through southern Italy, gathering support wherever they went. Despite being armed only with old-fashioned muskets, by the end of the year the Red Shirts had liberated Naples and Sicily and were marching on Rome. Cavour had been happy to let Garibaldi do the legwork in the south, but he couldn't risk him conquering the Papal States and alienating every Catholic monarch across Europe. He also didn't want Garibaldi to steal the credit for unification, so he quickly moved Sardinian troops into place, outmaneuvering the general. Cavour called Garibaldi "a savage," while Garibaldi referred to the Prime Minister as "a low intriguer," but in 1860 when Garibaldi finally met Victor he shook his hand, greeting him as King of Italy. He always refused to accept any reward for his services.

ABOVE & RIGHT
*The smooth-talking aristocratic Cavour (above)
became the first Prime Minister of a unified Italy but
died after just three months in office. Garibaldi (right)
rides into Naples on horseback in 1860, looking for
all the world like a cowboy from the Wild West.*

became a figurehead for the rising nationalist movement, the Risorgimento. There was one issue on which the two disagreed, however: Rosa. Cavour believed that the man who planned to lead a unified Italy should not have such a stain on his character. After Adelaide's death, foreign monarchs began proposing new candidates for Victor to marry: Queen Victoria suggested Princess Mary Adelaide of Cambridge; Napoleon III had proposed a German princess; and Cavour himself favored a Russian grand-duchess. All of these would bring significant political advantages, but Victor was adamant that he did not want to remarry. Cavour ordered that Rosa be followed to see whether she was being unfaithful to the King—of course, she wasn't—and threw his support behind Laura Bon, another of Victor's mistresses. She was of better breeding, but she couldn't oust the favorite, as Cavour had hoped. Rosa bore the slights with fortitude because she couldn't deny her lowly birth, but Victor frequently became incensed on her behalf. One day, after he had given the King yet another lecture on the subject, Cavour received a note requesting that he come to the palace that evening. When he arrived, he found Rosa sitting on the King's knee, and Victor said sternly, "You have forced me to make it clear to you that Rosina and I will love each other forever."

He explained his position in a letter to Jérome Bonaparte, Prince of Montfort: "A word of honor binds me to this woman. I will not marry any other woman, and I will marry her when it becomes possible, but I will not say when." Of course, Rosa must have dreamed of being queen, especially when she had to put up with all the veiled insults and slights of the nobility, but she did not nag her beloved. He took good care of her and her children, and that was enough.

In April 1859, Victor made Rosa the Countess of Mirafiori and Fontanafredda, and later that year he asked her to follow when he rode into battle against the Austrians. She was by his side as the papal army was driven back to the Vatican City and very distressed when the Pope excommunicated Victor for this conquest. The couple arrived in Naples after Giuseppe Garibaldi's successful campaign brought down the monarchy there and on March 17, 1861, when Victor became King of a unified Italy and Turin was proclaimed capital, Rosa was again behind the scenes. They were as close as any married couple could have been, and lived happily together in Turin, away from the intrigues of the Florentine court. From time to time, Victor took other mistresses, and even had children with them, but

ABOVE
*Victor Emmanuel's
troops march into Florence
during the Wars of Italian
Unification. His court
was based there from
1864 until 1870, when
he relocated to Rome.*

Rosa was always the firm favorite. In 1866, their son fought in the
Third Italian War of Independence and was honored for his brave
conduct on the battlefield, while for their daughter Victor arranged
a prestigious marriage to his aide-de-camp, the Marquis Giacomo
Filippo Spinola. But although Rosa and Victor were very happy, she
still had to put up with those who called her the king's whore, usually
behind her back but sometimes to her face.

A MORGANATIC MARRIAGE

In 1869, the King was struck down with an illness so severe that
it appeared as though he would not survive. He was given the holy
sacrament, but the priest sent to him by the Archbishop of Pisa told
him that in order to gain absolution, he must marry Rosa, the woman
with whom he lived in sin. On October 18, they were married by
a priest at his bedside, and soon afterward Victor began to recover.
He made it very clear to Rosa that although she was his wife, it was
a morganatic marriage and she was not Queen of Italy. The Italian
people would never have accepted their royal family being diluted
with peasant blood. For her part, she was simply happy that at last he
had made an honest woman of her. In 1870, after General Garibaldi

liberated Rome from papal hands, Victor gave Rosa a large villa in the city's Via Nomentana, a place that would become a refuge for him from the headache of tying up all the loose ends left after unification.

Still, they had not been married in a civil ceremony. It would be November 7, 1877, before Victor Emmanuel tied up that particular loose end. Then on January 5, 1878, he heard that Rosa was ill at their country estate and wanted to rush to her but was too unwell himself. She was unable to come to him either, though their two children were at his bedside when on January 9, he passed away. It transpired that he had been having secret communications with the Pope with the goal of being welcomed back into the Roman Catholic Church, but the details had not been concluded, which upset Rosa terribly. She lived for almost eight more years in the seclusion of the Villa Nomentana, desperately missing her glorious king.

Their relationship may have begun because the young Victor was bowled over by her physical beauty, but it lasted for thirty years because of the beauty of her character. She always remained honest and straightforward, while in return he was loyal to her and her family, even though she was not his only mistress. Being close to such a natural person from a lowly background kept Victor in touch with his subjects and may well have made him a better king.

THE PANTHEON

The tombs of two Italian kings lie in the magnificent 2nd-century Pantheon in Rome: those of Victor Emanuel II and the son who succeeded him, Umberto I. Umberto's queen got to rest alongside him but Victor's first family would not allow Rosa to join him there. Instead her children had a mausoleum built for her near Turin, which is similar in design to the Pantheon but on a much smaller scale. The Pantheon is a circular, domed building with a hole in the roof, the oculus. When it rains, water sprays onto the congregation below, and drains off to the sides. It was built by Roman Emperor Marcus Agrippa, and the name comes from the Greek Pantheos, meaning "all gods." The Pantheon is one of most impressive royal burial sites in the world, along with the Pyramids of Giza, the Taj Mahal, London's Westminster Abbey, Ulysses S. Grant's Tomb in New York, and Lenin's Mausoleum in Red Square, Moscow. It shows how much Italians valued King Victor Emmanuel—unlike his great-grandson, Umberto II, who they deposed, in 1946, thereafter abolishing the monarchy.

LEFT
The Pantheon's magnificent dome.

Rudolph, Crown Prince of Austria

– & –

Baroness Mary Vetsera

Rudolph Franz Karl Joseph von Habsburg–Lorraine
Born: August 21, 1858, Laxenburg, Austria
Died: January 30, 1889, Mayerling, Austria

Marie "Mary" Alexandrina von Vetsera
Born: March 19, 1871, Vienna, Austria
Died: January 30, 1889, Mayerling, Austria

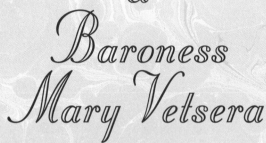

Mary had been brought up by an ambitious, social-climbing mother who was determined that she would marry well, so an heir to the Austro-Hungarian throne would have seemed like a perfect match. Prince Rudolph, however, was depressed, dissolute, thirteen years older than the impressionable Mary—and already married.

*A*s the only son of Emperor Franz Joseph I and Empress Elizabeth, Rudolph was expected to perpetuate the Hapsburg family's rule over the Austrian Empire, which covered a vast area from Italy in the south to Poland in the north and out to the Balkans in the east. Soon after his birth, his father proclaimed him to be "not exactly beautiful, but well built and strong," and the royal heir was given the rank of colonel in the Imperial Austrian Army while still a baby. Rudolph was educated by a string of tutors and early on showed himself to be very intelligent, with a mastery of several languages, including German, Hungarian, Czech, and English. He had a philosophical bent and enjoyed intellectual debate on subjects such as religion and politics, showing a maturity of understanding beyond his years. He had a passion for natural sciences and began his own mineral collection, and he also developed a taste for hunting.

ABOVE
Emperor Franz Joseph was an old-fashioned ruler of the type that was dying out in Europe. Throughout his sixty-eight-year reign, he struggled to hold the empire together.

As a teenager, Rudolph began to question his father's conservative, iron-fisted style of rule and, inspired by the French Revolution and the various popular revolts that had swept Europe in 1848, he began to consider more liberal, progressive types of monarchy. He yearned to continue his studies at university, but his father decided that he had received quite enough education by the age of eighteen and instructed him to join the army. Rudolph was stationed in Prague, a city of which he grew very fond. He enjoyed the routine of military life and entered into a few affairs of the heart, including one with a beautiful Jewish girl who fell ill and died, leaving him haunted by her memory.

OPPOSITE
Rudolph as a young boy (inset) and as a thirty-year-old man wearing hunting gear. According to court protocol, his mother was not allowed much of a role in his upbringing and his father, although delighted to have an heir, was a distant figure.

As heir to the throne it was essential that Rudolph make a suitable marriage, so a list of candidates was drawn up when he was twenty-one years old. The girl had to be from a European royal family and also Catholic, which limited the field somewhat, but Rudolph was happy to propose to Stéphanie, daughter of King Leopold II of Belgium.

> "*In Stéphanie I have found a real angel, a faithful good being who loves me*"

He went to Brussels to meet her in March 1880 and wrote afterward, "In Stéphanie I have found a real angel, a faithful good being who loves me." In fact, she was only fifteen, rather clumsy, and not nearly as well-educated as he was. Rudolph's mother was against the match, recognizing they had little in common, but she was unable to change his mind.

The marriage took place on May 10, 1881, and was attended by European royalty, including Prince Edward, heir to the British throne. Rudolph and Stéphanie honeymooned in Laxenburg Castle just outside Vienna, a cold, draughty place where, according to Stéphanie's memoirs, her new husband deflowered her in a crude, decidedly unromantic way. It was an inauspicious start to a marriage and, on their return to Vienna, Rudolph was preoccupied with his military career and his friendships with political activists and writers, leaving Stéphanie alone for long periods. She struggled to fit in with the rules of etiquette at the Viennese court and was nicknamed *"dass Trapeltier"* (the clumsy oaf) by the Empress Elizabeth. However, in letters to friends Rudolph spoke fondly of his wife, especially when in September 1883 she gave birth to a daughter, whom they named Elisabeth. For several years their letters were affectionate, even loving—"I am longing for you and count the days which still separate us," he wrote in August 1885— but, as his mother had recognized, their personalities were quite different, and perhaps it was inevitable that they would drift apart. Their estrangement left a vacancy in the life of the imaginative, romantic Rudolph; he needed someone to feel close to, someone to love.

BELOW
The wedding of Stéphanie and Rudolph on May 10, 1881. According to a friend, he had second thoughts the night before the ceremony but felt it was too late to pull out.

GHEMAR FRÈRES
PHOTOGRAPHIE BRUXELLES INALTÉRABLE (Déposé)

BLINDED BY LOVE

There had been rumors about Rudolph's dissolute lifestyle since he was a teenager, although many were undoubtedly exaggerated. He certainly took opium and was known to be a hard drinker, as a result of which by his late twenties he was beginning to lose the handsome looks of his youth. There wasn't a particularly strong moral code at the Viennese court and affairs were common in aristocratic circles. All the same, Stéphanie must have been devastated when her husband gave her a venereal disease, thought to be syphilis. As a result, she had to have a gynecological operation, which made it unlikely she would bear any further children—meaning Rudolph would not have the son he needed to continue the Hapsburg dynasty. Stéphanie went to a spa in the summer of 1887 in an attempt to regain her fertility, but to no avail. The strain on their marriage must have been immense.

Around this time, Rudolph met Mizzi Kaspar, an attractive, vivacious woman who worked as an actress and dancer. He lavished money on her and she was happy to become a royal mistress—although she was rather a disloyal one who reported back to a police informer about the Crown Prince's movements. According to friends, Mizzi became the great love of Rudolph's life, but there was another young woman in Vienna who had set her sights on him, though they had yet to be introduced.

Mary Vetsera was the daughter of an elderly baron who worked as a diplomat for the Austrian court, and a Greek mother who came from a prominent banking family. As such, they were not part of the

ABOVE
A lively, happy girl who worked as an actress and dancer, Mizzi Kaspar was said to be the love of Rudolph's life.

BELOW
The Hofburg Palace in Vienna, pictured c. 1890. The royal family tended to stay there in winter, then move for the summer to the Schönbrunn Palace, to enjoy its extensive gardens.

THE ROYAL PROCURESS

Born Marie Louise Mendel, the Countess Larisch was Rudolph's first cousin, the daughter of Empress Elizabeth's brother. The Empress arranged her marriage to Count Georg Larisch when she was nineteen years old but it was an unhappy union from the start. They had five children, but it's said only two of them were fathered by the count, and he never gave the Countess enough money so she was forced to turn to her cousin Rudolph for handouts, even though they had never been particularly close. The Countess was thirty years old and should have known better when she introduced young Mary Vetsera to the Crown Prince. According to her memoirs, published in 1913, she had warned her, "Wolves like Rudolph eat up little lambs like you." But still she continued to facilitate the relationship by pretending to chaperone the young girl while delivering her into the arms of her seducer. When Empress Elizabeth found out about the Countess's role in the scandal surrounding Rudolph and Mary, she was banished from the royal court. Her memoirs seek to exonerate her, but most historians question their veracity.

RIGHT
Countess Larisch (left) with Mary Vetsera.

established aristocratic set in Vienna and were not introduced at court, although they lived in a luxurious home in which they often held glamorous parties. Mary's mother hoped to raise the family's prestige by forming advantageous marriages for her three daughters. Mary had been educated at an "Institute for Daughters of the Nobility," where she learned social graces such as music, drawing, and conversing in French. Both of her sisters had married counts and Mary was expected to do at least as well. According to the memoirs of her friend, Countess Marie Larisch, she complained: "Mamma has no love for me . . . Ever since I was a little girl she has treated me as something she means to dispose of to the best advantage." By the autumn of 1887, the family had an understanding with Duke Miguel of Braganza, a member of the royal family of Portugal, that Mary would be married to him in due course. However, she had already developed her crush on Crown Prince Rudolph, whose picture she pored over. His melancholy appearance touched her, making her yearn to be the one person who could save him, and she nagged the Duke of Braganza, who often went hunting with Rudolph, to tell her all about him. When she spotted him once at the races, she commented to her maid how handsome he was.

According to Countess Larisch, Mary's obsession grew and in spring 1888 she wrote a letter to her idol, who replied suggesting they should meet. Mary must have been beside herself with excitement but word of it reached the ears of her mother, who immediately shipped the seventeen-year-old girl to England for the summer months. Far from quelling her passion, Mary was keener than ever when she returned to Vienna in the fall. She wrote to a former governess, Hermine, "Do not believe that I have forgotten him. I only love him much more dearly." According to her letters, she was finally introduced to the Prince in the Prater, an amusement park near the Danube, by the Countess Larisch. The Countess then took her to the Prince's rooms at the Palace on November 5, 1888, having lied to the girl's mother that they were going shopping together. Mary wrote to her governess, overjoyed with the meeting: "Today you will get a happy letter because I have been with him."

> "Do not believe that I have forgotten him. I only love him much more dearly"

When Mary wandered into Rudolph's life on that day in the winter of 1888, he was thirty years old and depressed. He could only watch as his father, the Emperor, made decisions that he thought would be disastrous and would ruin any chances of his own reign being successful. Rudolph was clever and opinionated but had no actual power. He was prone to severe headaches and seizures, probably as a result of his drug and alcohol abuse, and he saw the life stretching ahead of him as empty and worthless. The pretty, young, adoring Mary provided a refuge. She was empty-headed and knew nothing of politics, but she was warm and undemanding, and Rudolph couldn't help but be flattered by the young girl's adoration. He was still in love with Mizzi, but Mary was an extremely attractive alternative. Stéphanie's sister later described her as "an imperial sultana" with "her deep black eyes, her cameo-like profile, her throat of a goddess, and her arresting sensual grace." Having won the attention of her hero, Mary wasn't going to let him slip through her fingers. No matter what he asked of her, she was determined to do it.

BELOW
Mary was a well-brought-up girl and her mother was furious to hear she had sent Rudolph an engraved cigarette case. "She is compromising herself when she is scarcely seventeen years old and so is ruining not only her life but also that of her brothers and sisters and mother."

A DOOMED ROMANCE

Once the Countess Larisch had quit Vienna, it became harder for Mary and Rudolph to meet because it was unheard of for a girl of her social station to be unchaperoned. But at least Mary's maid and Rudolph's valet could still convey their letters to each other. As she wrote to Hermine, "Since I have met him and talked to him my love has so much deepened. I ponder day and night how I could contrive to see him." On December 11, the Vienna Opera began to perform Wagner's Ring Cycle, which Mary's mother and sister attended religiously. Mary found excuses not to accompany them and instead spent the evenings with Rudolph, timing her return by the length of the opera. "He is my god, my everything," she wrote to her governess, and it seemed Rudolph was beginning to share her feelings. He gave her an iron wedding ring, which she wore on a chain around her neck. On the inside, he had engraved the letters ILVBIDT, which he explained meant, *"In Liebe vereint bis in den Tod"* ("United in love till death"). Mary began to entertain the idea that they might one day be married. "If we could only live together in a hut, we would be so happy!" she wrote to her governess—but at the same time she recognized this was not a possibility for the heir to the throne.

Several people remarked on Rudolph's low spirits around this time. His mother was worried that he looked ill and tired. One of his army colleagues reported that whenever he heard of the death of someone, Rudolph would remark, "He is fortunate." But the biggest clue to his state of mind comes from the testimony of Mizzi Kaspar, whom he had continued to see despite his new relationship. According to her, Rudolph had mentioned several times during the summer of 1888 that he might shoot himself and in December he asked if she would come into the Vienna Woods with him where they could both commit suicide. She laughed off the suggestion. At twenty-four years old, she led a charmed life as an actress and royal mistress and had no intention of ending it prematurely. After her refusal, Rudolph turned to Mary instead and in mid-January they consummated their relationship. Afterwards she wrote to her governess, "We both have lost our heads. Now we belong to each other life and soul."

It seems that Rudolph may have broached the subject of divorce with his father, but the reaction was a vehement refusal even to consider the idea. This could have been the final straw that made him determine to end his life. Certainly, by January 27, everyone at an evening reception at the court noticed that Rudolph seemed terribly

depressed and that relations between him and his father were markedly
cool. Mary was present but she left early with her mother and Rudolph
went to spend the night with Mizzi Kaspar, to whom he had recently
given the large sum of 60,000 *gulden*. During those last days of January,
he spent his time destroying his personal papers and correspondence,
and settling his affairs. His mind was made up.

On January 28, Rudolph left for Mayerling, his hunting lodge
in the woods southwest of Vienna. Mary sneaked away during an
afternoon's outing with the Countess Larisch, and joined him later
that day. It's not clear whether she had already agreed to end her life
beside the man to whom she was utterly devoted, but the Countess
Larisch certainly thought so and claimed she tried to alert the police.
No one intervened, though, and late at night on the 29th, Mary sat in

> *"We are both going blissfully into the uncertain beyond ... Since I could not resist love, I am going with him"*

bed writing farewell letters to her family, giving instructions that she should be buried with Rudolph and asking her sister to lay a gardenia on her grave every year. "We are both going blissfully into the uncertain beyond," she wrote to her sister. "Since I could not resist love, I am going with him." Rudolph's short, factual letters were already written and sealed. In the early hours of the morning, Mary was shot in the temple with a revolver—whether by her own hand or Rudolph's is not clear. A damp handkerchief she was clutching suggested she had been crying. Rudolph remained with her body for some hours, speaking to one of the servants at half past six, and only then did he pull the trigger and fulfill his own part in their suicide pact.

Did Rudolph love Mary? In his farewell letter to his mother, he referred to her as a "pure angel who accompanied him into the other world." His letters say that by dying he hopes to save his name, but he doesn't ever say he is doing it for love. Mary fulfilled a purpose for him, simply keeping him company. Blinded by love, she threw her young life away for the sake of an emotionally unstable, drug-addicted, married man.

ABOVE
The last photograph of Mary, wearing the clothes in which she would later be buried.

RIGHT
Rudolph lying in state with a bandage covering the gunshot wounds to his head. His skull had been reconstructed with wax to give it a normal appearance.

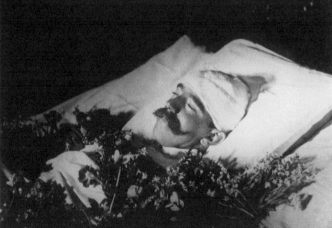

MYSTERIES OF MAYERLING

The servant who found Rudolph's body believed he had been poisoned by potassium cyanide, possibly administered by Mary. The royal family released a story to the press that he had died of an aneurysm, and they forced Mary's family to bury her secretly at a nearby monastery. However, too many servants had seen the bodies and the suicide notes for details to be kept secret and news of the pact slipped out. Those who committed suicide were not permitted to be buried in sacred ground, but a special dispensation was obtained from the Pope to bury Rudolph in the family tomb because, they argued, he had been suffering from an inherited form of madness, which came from his mother's side of the family. Rumors surrounding the deaths were rife: some speculated that Rudolph had been about to side with Hungarian rebels against his father and backed out at the last moment; wilder stories circulated that the Emperor had ordered their deaths, or even that the couple had been killed by French spies. Mary's remains were taken from her grave in 1991 by a man who was obsessed by the affair, and according to the private forensic report he commissioned no evidence of a gunshot was found; others argue the hundred-year-old skeleton was not hers. The only two people who could have told the whole story died the night of January 30, 1889.

BELOW
The Mayerling lodge, c. 1889, as it was when Rudolph and Mary died there.

Emperor & Autocrat of All the Russias
& Empress Consort of Russia

Nicholas II
– & –
Alexandra

Nikolai Alexandrovich Romanov
Born: May 18, 1868, Tsarskoye Selo, Russia
Died: July 17, 1918, Yekaterinburg, Russia

**Victoria Alix Helena Louise Beatrice
(later Alexandra Feodorovna)**
Born: June 6, 1872, Darmstadt, German Empire
Died: July 17, 1918, Yekaterinburg, Russia

Married: November 26, 1894

Nicholas grew up with the conviction that he
must one day maintain the autocracy

"I sat next to little twelve-year-old Alix, whom I really liked a lot,"
wrote Nicholas, sixteen-year-old heir to the Russian throne, in his diary.
Theirs was an innocent meeting on May 27, 1884, when she came to
St. Petersburg for her older sister's wedding, but it would end in a
tragedy that would shock and horrify the world.

As a child, Nicholas was quiet and good-natured, and loved
playing outdoors with his younger brother, George. Their
father, Alexander III, was a strict disciplinarian who tried to
toughen up his son, so their relationship was strained, but Nicholas
was close to his mother, and the main influence in his early years was
a string of tutors who taught him the importance of his role as heir of
the Romanov dynasty and future tsar of Russia. Nicholas's family was
related to several European monarchies, including the British dynasty
of Queen Victoria, who was grandmother to his mother's cousin, the
future George V; in fact, during a visit when Nicholas was just five,
he developed a crush on Princess Victoria, George's sister.

Then, at the age of thirteen, Nicholas's world was shaken when his
grandfather, Tsar Alexander II, was assassinated by a terrorist bomb.
The Tsar was brought back to the Winter Palace in St. Petersburg
and Nicholas watched in horror as doctors tried desperately to save
him, to no avail. Soon after the Tsar's death, Alexander III was sworn
in and, as the new Tsar, the supreme ruler of Russia, he vowed he
would never give in to rebels and would crush all enemies. Alexander
III decided there was no need for young Nicholas to be taught
about affairs of state until he reached the age of thirty, because he,
Alexander, intended to rule until old age. This meant that Nicholas
grew up with the conviction that he must one day maintain the
autocracy, but had no education in how that might best be achieved.
It was this decision to keep Nicholas in the dark that would later lead
to tragedy for the Romanovs.

A CHILDHOOD ROMANCE

Alix of Hesse was a pretty girl whose nickname was "Sunny," because
as a baby she was always smiling. Her father was Grand Duke of
Hesse and her mother Alice was the second daughter of Queen

OPPOSITE
*Nicholas II in the 1890s.
He was a weak man who
tended to procrastinate rather
than take action. When a
telegram was brought telling
him that the Russian Pacific
fleet had been wiped out, he
stuffed it in his pocket and
continued playing tennis.*

"Alix and I wrote our names on a window (we love each other)"

Victoria. She grew up in Darmstadt until tragedy struck the family in November 1878, when all but one member of her family, her older sister Ella, contracted diphtheria, resulting in the deaths of her mother and youngest sister. From then on, Alix was raised in England, where Queen Victoria personally oversaw her education. When Nicholas first met her, at the wedding of her sister Ella to his uncle Sergei, she was wearing a white muslin dress and had roses in her hair, a sight he would always remember. The children played together after the ceremony and a few days later Nicholas tried to give Alix a gift of a brooch. Embarrassed, she returned it, but they continued to grow closer. He wrote in his diary during her visit, "Alix and I wrote our names on a window (we love each other)." Both were romantic souls who felt a common bond and were sad when she had to return to England.

Five years later, when Alix was seventeen, she received a proposal of marriage from Prince Albert Victor, the eldest son of the Prince of Wales. He was second in line of succession to the British throne, but still she refused him. Was it because she was hankering after Nicholas? Certainly, when she visited her sister Ella in St. Petersburg that summer, she and Nicholas were almost inseparable, going to concerts and balls by night and ice-skating by day. It was obvious they were in love; however, the match was unpopular. Queen Victoria was fond of the girl and didn't want her to move to Russia, fearing it might not be safe, while Tsar Alexander objected because Alix had been brought up a Lutheran while they were Russian Orthodox. Besides, Russian society had not taken to Alix during her visit, finding her dowdy and uncharismatic. Alexander hoped that once she returned to England, the romance would fade. They were still young. There was plenty of time for both to meet someone else.

A FUNERAL, A WEDDING, AND A CORONATION

In 1890 Tsar Alexander contrived to have Nicholas introduced to Mathilde Kschessinska, a leading Russian ballerina. They began a passionate affair but in his diary Nicholas still wrote of his yearning for Alix: "My dream is to one day marry Alix H. . . . For a long time I resisted my feeling that my dream will come true." Opportunities to see each other were few and far between, and it wasn't until the spring of 1894, when they met in Coburg for the wedding of Alix's brother, that Nicholas saw his a chance to propose. When his father refused to give permission for the match, Nicholas declared that if he could not marry Alix, then he would not marry at all. This would have been catastrophic for the dynasty because there would have been no heir, so Alexander had to relent—but there was yet another obstacle. When Nicholas asked Alix for her hand in marriage, she was torn between her love for him and her reluctance to give up her religion and convert to Russian Orthodoxy. The young lovers discussed it for hours on end, and Queen Victoria, relenting when she realized how much they loved each other, conceded that the two churches weren't significantly different and that Alix should go with her heart. When Alix finally agreed to marry him, Nicholas wrote in his diary, "A marvellous, unforgettable day! Oh God, what a mountain has rolled from my shoulders."

BELOW
Alix of Hesse was a strong character who dominated her husband. Her life revolved around him and their five children, especially as she found no friends among the Russian nobility.

A month later, Nicholas traveled to England to visit Alix, bringing with him many engagement presents, one of them a beautiful Fabergé sapphire-and-diamond brooch. In her fiancé's diary, Alix wrote, "You are locked in my heart, the little key is lost and now you must stay there forever." They were overjoyed to be together at last, but when Nicholas returned to Russia bad news awaited him: his father had become seriously ill with a kidney infection and the outlook was bleak. Alix left quickly for Russia to support her fiancé and to receive her father-in-law's blessing as his condition worsened. The entire family clustered around the bedside for ten days until, on November 1, 1894, Alexander died.

THE CORONATION OF NICHOLAS & ALEXANDRA

Royal coronation ceremonies are always glittering occasions but Russian ones were particularly lavish, steeped in all the ceremony of the Russian Orthodox church. They were held at the Cathedral of the Dormition in Moscow, and by tradition the Tsar had to stay elsewhere the night before and enter the city on the morning of the Coronation. Nicholas and Alexandra arrived in a procession of gilt coaches and were ushered in by the high clergy. As Nicholas approached the altar steps, the Chain of the Order of St. Andrew, a ceremonial necklace representing Russia's highest order of chivalry, broke, but the news was covered up as it was seen as a bad omen. All the ladies present were dripping with emeralds, sapphires, and diamonds, and the altar screen of the Cathedral was decorated with gold, silver, and priceless icons.

Nicholas and Alexandra walked under separate canopies to their thrones; his was set with 870 diamonds. Nicholas was crowned first with the diamond-encrusted Imperial Crown, which weighed nine pounds, then Alexandra received the lighter Consort's Crown. The Tsar was anointed with holy oils and received Holy Communion before taking the coronation oath. After the hours-long ceremony, bells pealed and cannon fired out across the city, then 7,000 guests sat down to a sumptuous banquet.

BELOW & RIGHT
The Coronation of Nicholas and Alexandra, May 26, 1896.
Their coaches proceeded through the streets of Moscow before
the ceremony (below). After being crowned, Nicholas kissed
his mother, the Dowager Empress (right).

Nicholas and Alix had planned to marry the following spring, but he asked her to bring forward the wedding because he couldn't bear to be separated from her, given the weight of his new responsibilities. The next morning, Alix was received into the Russian Orthodox Church and a week after the old Tsar's funeral, on November 26, Nicholas and Alix, now renamed the Grand Duchess Alexandra Feodorovna, were married in the Winter Palace. "One day in deepest mourning, lamenting a loved one, the next in smartest clothes being married," Alexandra described it in a letter to her sister. Crowds cheered as they left the palace after the ceremony. As they began their married life at the Alexander Palace in Tsarskoe Selo, Nicholas wrote in his diary, "There are no words capable of describing the bliss it is to be living together." Their joy intensified when Alexandra gave birth to a daughter, Olga, in November 1895.

> "There are no words capable of describing the bliss it is to be living together"

Their coronation took place on May 26, 1896, with a lavish ceremony. The following day, according to custom, citizens were invited to an open-air feast with free beer and gifts of enamel cups for all. A crowd of 100,000 gathered, but the atmosphere turned ugly when it became apparent that there weren't enough cups to go around. A stampede ensued in which an estimated 1,389 died and 1,300 were injured. When Nicholas heard the awful news, he wanted to cancel the ball scheduled for that evening at the French Embassy, but his advisors begged him to attend so as not to offend the French. As a result, he offended his own citizens, and the Russian people began to turn against him and his German bride for attending festivities while so many of his citizens lay dying.

A SICKLY HEIR

Nicholas and Alexandra were blissfully happy in the early years of his reign. Why wouldn't they be? They had each other, and money was no object as she redecorated the sumptuous Winter Palace in St. Petersburg and their home at Tsarskoe Selo with fine paintings, crystal chandeliers, and priceless antiques. They had three more daughters, Tatiana, Marie, and Anastasia, then in August 1904 a son was born who would be heir to the Romanov dynasty. Nicholas wrote in his diary, "A great, never-to-be-forgotten day." Celebrations were held to mark the birth of baby Alexis Nikolaevich, political

ABOVE

*Alexis, aged five. He was
said to be a serious boy with
a heart of gold, known to his
parents and sisters as "Baby."*

ABOVE RIGHT

*The Romanov family in
1914. Standing, from left to
right, are the two older girls,
Olga and Tatiana. Sitting
are Marie, Alexandra, Tsar
Nicholas, and Anastasia,
with little Alexis in front.*

prisoners were freed, and huge sums of money were donated to charity. But his parents' joy was short-lived, because when he was less than two months old his mother noticed bleeding from the baby's navel and she began to suspect he suffered from hemophilia, the dreaded, incurable disease her uncle and her brother had suffered from, which stopped the blood from clotting. As the child started crawling, doctors confirmed her suspicions as he developed swellings after any slight bump or knock. Alexandra considered herself responsible because the condition was inherited from her family, and she was inconsolable. Nicholas was worried but tried to reassure her that the boy would have the best care doctors could provide.

Meanwhile, Nicholas was proving clumsy and inept as a leader. He had already mishandled relations with Japan so badly that a war ensued in 1904, resulting in the annihilation of the Russian Pacific fleet. Then in 1905, when a priest called George Gapon marched with 120,000 workers to the Winter Palace to hand a petition to the Tsar asking for more civil rights, soldiers opened fire, killing 92 and wounding several hundred. The day became known as Bloody Sunday. It was a serious miscalculation that led to Gapon calling for an armed uprising against the monarchy. There were countrywide strikes and protests, the Black Sea fleet mutinied, terrorist bombs exploded, and the economy ground to a halt as the government struggled to regain control. Nicholas tried to stick to the principle of autocracy that had been drummed into him in boyhood, but by October he had no choice but to sign a manifesto drawn up by his prime minister, Sergei Witte, giving the vote to all Russian men and creating a Duma (a form of government) that would limit the power of the monarch.

Nicholas and Alexandra tried to keep young Alexis's condition a secret but rumors leaked out that he was not in robust health. In 1912, he suffered internal bleeding after jumping out of a boat. The eight-year-old boy was in a lot of pain and as he grew weaker, his distraught mother, clutching at every straw, asked for the help of a controversial faith healer from Siberia by the name of Grigory Rasputin. Rasputin sent her a telegram, which read, "The little one will not die. Do not allow the doctors to bother him too much." The next day her son began to recover. Alexandra was convinced that Rasputin had cured him with his prayers, and he soon became a regular visitor to the imperial court, advising Alexandra on little Alexis's care. He was wild-looking with a depraved reputation, and rumors spread in Russian society that he was Alexandra's lover and that he had bewitched her. She had never made strong friendships amongst the Russian nobility, partly because she was shy and also because her command of the language was poor, so there was no one to defend her. Successive prime ministers warned Nicholas against Rasputin but he was persuaded by his wife's convictions that the healer was the best hope of saving their son. It was a fatal mistake, as the Russian people came to believe that Rasputin's mystical influence over the royal couple was growing and affecting decisions of state.

GRIGORY RASPUTIN

Rasputin was born a peasant in a small Siberian village, and had no schooling, but from an early age he was a commanding presence with a forceful personality. As a young man, he traveled to Greece and the Holy Land, studying different belief systems, and on his return to Russia slowly built his reputation as a psychic and faith healer. He was first introduced to Alexandra by the Bishop of Saratov and, after he appeared to heal their son Alexis, became part of the royal entourage. He was a controversial figure, with a voracious appetite for alcohol and sex, who was not above telling women that sexual contact with him could cure their illnesses. According to legend, Rasputin's murderers struggled to kill him—a story that contributed to the belief that Rasputin possessed other-worldly powers. First they poisoned him, then they stabbed and shot him repeatedly, yet still he was alive until they wrapped him in a carpet and drowned him in a freezing river.

LEFT
Rasputin, the mad monk, was seen by Russians as a dark, mystical force bent on destroying their country.

THE END OF THE TSARS

Russia was dragged into the First World War in 1914, and the army was soon faring badly. In 1916 Nicholas went to the front to assume control, leaving the unpopular Alexandra in charge back in Russia. She fired some trusted commanders and replaced them with candidates favored by Rasputin, and rumors spread that she was on Germany's side in the war. Discontent increased until in December 1916 a group of nobles murdered Rasputin to try and salvage the reputation of the monarchy, but it was too late. Alexandra was devastated by the killing, and continued to maintain that Rasputin had been a good friend to their family. Food shortages ensued from her mismanagement and in March 1917 riots broke out across St. Petersburg. Nicholas sent troops to quell them, but instead his soldiers joined the rioters, so fed up were they with two rulers who appeared so inept and self-serving. The army and the government called on Nicholas to abdicate and on March 17, realizing all other options were closed to him, he renounced the throne in favor of his son Alexis. He then changed his mind, considering his child's illness, and instead offered power to his brother Michael, who declined it. On March 21, the terrified Alexandra was placed under arrest by a provisional government and when Nicholas returned to Tsarskoe Selo, his entire family, heirs of the great Romanov dynasty, were taken prisoner by revolutionary guards.

Alexandra spent the days of captivity indoors, knitting and caring for her children. Nicholas ventured out daily for some exercise, either clearing snow or riding his bicycle, but was treated with increasing contempt by the guards who patrolled the grounds, once even being knocked off his bike by them. Meanwhile, the revolutionary government debated what to do with the family. Some advocated putting Nicholas on trial, while others thought they should be exiled to England.

BELOW
Due to land reforms, by 1905 Russian peasants found themselves unable to make a living and roamed the countryside looking for work. As a New York newspaper points out, this was one of the causes of the 1905 Revolution.

New-York Tribune.

PART II.   SUNDAY, DECEMBER 10, 1905.   EIGHT PAGES.

TYPES OF THE RUSSIAN COMMON PEOPLE NOW IN A STATE OF REVOLT.

In August, they were moved to the governor's mansion in Tobolsk, where they lived in comfort while awaiting their fate. In October, power was seized by the Bolsheviks, a mass organization of workers led by Vladimir Ilyich Lenin, but Nicholas had never heard of him and did not realize this was a dangerous new development.

In May 1918, Lenin ordered that Nicholas, Alexandra, and their family be moved to the town of Yekaterinburg. He had probably already decided their fate by this stage, but his plans were set in stone when the anti-Communist Czech White Army invaded central Russia that month. The Bolsheviks were determined to prevent the royal family being rescued. At midnight on the evening of July 16, Jacob Yurovsky, the leader of the secret police guarding them, ordered his men to awaken the family and hustle them down to a basement room, telling them they were being moved for their own safety. Nicholas, Alexandra, their four children, the family doctor, and three remaining servants were present. Chairs were brought for Alexandra and Alexis before armed men filed into the room and Yurovsky told them they had been sentenced to death. Nicholas only had time to cry, "What, what?" and throw his arm around his beloved wife before being shot several times in the chest. Alexandra was making the sign of the cross as she died, and the others fell in a hail of bullets and bayonet thrusts.

What became of the Romanovs remained a mystery until over seventy years later when their bodies were discovered in a rubble-filled pit north of Yekaterinburg. In July 1991, they were given a state funeral and finally laid to rest. Nicholas and Alexandra were not bad people; in fact, they did a lot of charity work for the poor and needy of Russia. However, they were isolated by their wealth and position, meaning Nicholas was unable to interpret and respond to the changing mood in his country, while Alexandra was too caught up in her family and her mystical beliefs to advise him effectively. Their intense love for each other sustained them during the days of captivity, as it had since that innocent meeting at a wedding thirty-two years earlier, but it couldn't save them from the rise of Communism and the anger of the Russian people.

ABOVE
Nicholas II (top) shoveling snow on the grounds at Tsarskoe Selo, near St. Petersburg, where he and his family were held captive from March to August 1917. Alexandra (above) with her precious son, whose health was crucial for the future of the Romanov dynasty.

Duke & Duchess
of Windsor

Edward VIII
– & –
Wallis Simpson

Edward Albert Christian George Andrew Patrick David Windsor
Born: June 23, 1894, Richmond, England
Died: May 28, 1972, Paris, France

Bessie Wallis Warfield (later Wallis Simpson)
Born: June 19, 1896 (or 1895), Blue Ridge Summit, Pennsylvania
Died: April 24, 1986, Paris, France

Married: June 3, 1937

"*If I marry again, it will be for money*"

ABOVE

Edward, Prince of Wales, in 1930 (left). He was never out of the headlines, whether falling off a horse, dancing the Charleston or driving a steam train (all favorite pastimes). Wallis Simpson (right), famous for the quote, "You can never be too rich or too thin," was a self-contained, driven, and determined woman.

Like millions of other girls, the teenaged Wallis had a crush on the handsome Edward, Prince of Wales, whose picture regularly appeared in the newspapers. She had no idea then that she would ever meet him, never mind fall for him, and she certainly had no concept of the repercussions their love affair would have for the British throne.

Wallis's parents were unmarried when she was conceived and may not have been married when she was born near Baltimore in either 1895 or 1896 (she claimed it was 1896, which would make her legitimate, but some biographers disagree). Her father died of tuberculosis while she was still a baby and her mother had to rely on charity from the extended family to raise the little girl, who proved from a young age to be a determined, feisty character. In kindergarten, she hit a boy with a ruler because he butted in with the answer to a teacher's question that she had wanted to answer herself. At school she was known for being immaculately groomed, very stylish, and highly self-disciplined. Although not conventionally pretty, she was a lively conversationalist, who always gave her full attention to whomever she was speaking with, and perhaps for this reason she proved popular with the boys in her year.

In April 1916, Wallis visited Florida with friends and was introduced to US airman Earl Winfield Spencer, a handsome, confident man who fell passionately in love with her. They married quickly, in November the same year, but it wasn't long before she discovered her new husband was an alcoholic. After being caught flying while drunk, he was grounded and sent out to work in Hong Kong and China, where Wallis joined him in 1924. Various rumors concern her time there: that she became pregnant by an Italian lover and the subsequent termination made her infertile; and that she learned sex tricks in Chinese brothels to help men with low libidos. Certainly, both she and her husband took several lovers during the marriage and spent increasing amounts of time apart, until they divorced in 1927.

"If I marry again, it will be for money," Wallis told friends, just before she met Ernest Simpson, a partner in a shipping company. He was already married but Wallis began an affair with him and, according to his wife, lured him away during the winter of 1927/28 while she was ill in the hospital. In July 1928, Wallis and Ernest married at a register office in London, setting up home near Hyde Park. She was keen to inveigle her way into English society and used her connections to secure an introduction to Thelma, Lady Furness, then-mistress of Edward, the Prince of Wales. In January 1931, she obtained an invitation to a house party the Prince would be attending and contrived to sit next to him at the luncheon.

Edward's first words to her were, "You must miss central heating, Mrs. Simpson." It was a luxury English houses did not have at the time. "Every American woman who comes to England is asked that same question," she replied, her eyes sparkling. "I had hoped for something more original from the Prince of Wales." She had correctly divined that he was attracted to dominant women, and his interest in her was immediately piqued. It would be several months before they'd meet again, but there was no question Edward would remember her.

FROM COURTSHIP TO CRISIS

Edward grew up in the reign of Queen Victoria, his great-grandmother, very much aware that one day he would rule over Britain and its Empire, which at the time covered one-third of the world. His father was strict, regularly making the children line up so he could inspect their clothing and ensure they were impeccably presented. Edward was educated by nannies, then sent to naval college. During the First World War he served in the Grenadier Guards, earning a Military Cross in 1916. After the war he took on royal duties, representing his father, by then King George V, on many overseas visits. He was short at only five feet five inches tall, but women didn't seem to mind and, with his shock of blonde hair and playboy looks, he was a big hit wherever he went.

Edward was the most eligible bachelor of the 1920s and there were women galore, both mistresses and society ladies presented by ambitious mothers as potential brides. In January 1923. it was announced that he was to marry Elizabeth Bowes-Lyon, but he called it off and she went on to wed his brother Albert. There was talk of his marrying Princess Ileana of Romania, but it didn't come to anything. For many years after the war, he had an affair

ABOVE
*Wallis and Edward are
finally reunited near Tours
in April 1937 after four
months' separation during
which they communicated
by telephone and letter.*

with Freda Dudley Ward, a socialite who was married to a Liberal
member of parliament. While still involved with her, he met
American-born Thelma, Lady Furness, and they also became lovers,
although she gossiped behind his back about his lack of sexual
prowess, calling him "Little Man." There were many other affairs of
shorter duration and Edward's womanizing worried his father and the
prime minister, Stanley Baldwin, who hoped he would settle down
and find a sensible wife before inheriting the crown.

In 1931, when he met Wallis, Edward was thirty-six years old
and a fussy man who was keen on exercise and always immaculately
dressed, who enjoyed golf and dancing but felt very strongly his
responsibilities as heir to the throne. Their second meeting took place
in June 1931, after she had finagled an invitation to be presented at
court, and once again she challenged him, this time over a comment
he made about the lighting being unflattering to women. It was
January 1932 when she and Ernest received their first invitation
to Edward's home, Fort Belvedere, where she and Edward danced
together. "I found him a good dancer, deft, light on his feet, with a
true sense of rhythm," she wrote years later. There is no question that
she had set her sights on seducing him. He represented the epitome of

THE DUCHESS OF WINDSOR'S JEWELS

Wallis and Edward frequently gave each other lavish gifts, and were fond of jewelry from the top houses (especially Cartier), which they inscribed with personal messages. Edward's first gift, in the summer of 1934, was an emerald and diamond Cartier charm for Wallis's charm bracelet, followed by a Prince of Wales feathers diamond brooch in 1935. The engagement ring he gave her in 1936 was a gigantic emerald set in platinum with the inscription "We are ours now." A Cartier onyx and diamond panther bracelet and a gem-encrusted flamingo brooch reflected their taste for animal jewelry. A favorite piece was a Cartier cross bracelet, for which Edward gave Wallis new crosses to mark significant events: one was inscribed "Our Marriage Cross Wallis 3.VI.37 David"; an Appendectomy Cross was added after Wallis had the operation in 1944; and a "God Save the King" cross referred to Edward surviving an assassination attempt in 1936. In an auction at Sotheby's in 1987, the collection sold for $45 million.

RIGHT
Wallis's Cartier cross bracelet.

social success, and he was also very wealthy, while Ernest's company had fared badly in the Depression and money was tight. Wallis intensified her pursuit and in December 1933, while Thelma was back home in the United States, she succeeded in winning the Prince's heart. Thelma was furious but there was nothing she could do. Some speculate that Wallis had a strong sexual hold over the Prince (perhaps using those Chinese brothel tricks), others that he was enthralled by her dominant personality, but they obviously had a lot in common as well. During the summer of 1934, they traveled together through France and Spain; in the winter they went to Austria then Budapest. Edward bought her fabulous jewelry and gave her an allowance so that she could afford to dress in couture by her favorite designer, Mainbocher. Her husband, Ernest, by this time had a mistress of his own and did not object.

Wallis and Edward's affair continued through 1935, much to the distress of George V, who feared for the future of the throne if his son stuck with this twice-married and obviously unsuitable woman. Prime Minister Baldwin commissioned an intelligence report that uncovered Wallis's illegitimate birth, the fact that she hadn't been baptized, her many lovers, and her experiences

in China, among other insalubrious tales. Many witnesses reported that Wallis ordered Edward around, making him get down on his knees to fasten her shoes and treating him without the respect due to royalty. And then on January 20, 1936, George V slipped into a coma and died. The following day, in an act that broke with formal tradition, Wallis and Edward stood together at a window in York House to watch the ceremony that marked his accession to the throne.

BOTTOM
Relaxing on the Dalmatian coast of Croatia in summer 1936 before the abdication crisis blew up.

BELOW
The British press followed every ramification of the story, day by day.

THE DECISION OF A LIFETIME

By the summer of 1936, Edward had decided he wanted to marry Wallis and she had instituted divorce proceedings against Ernest. However, when he told the Prime Minister, Baldwin explained that it was impossible for them to marry because the Church of England was against divorce and the King was Head of the Church. He also told Edward that the British people would never accept Wallis

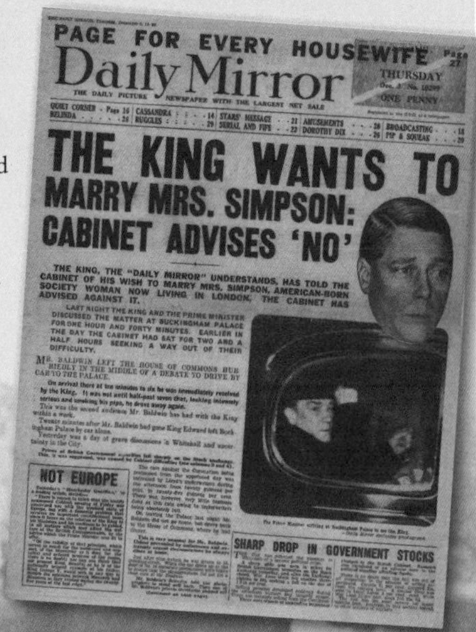

PAGE FOR EVERY HOUSEWIFE Page 27

Daily Mirror

THE DAILY PICTURE NEWSPAPER WITH THE LARGEST NET SALE

THURSDAY

ONE PENNY

QUIET CORNER - Page 16 | CASSANDRA - 14 | STARS' MESSAGE - 21 | AMUSEMENTS - 28 | BROADCASTING - 18
BELINDA - 26 | RUGGLES - 29 | SERIAL AND FIFE - 22 | DOROTHY DIX - 26 | PIP & SQUEAK - 29

THE KING WANTS TO MARRY MRS. SIMPSON: CABINET ADVISES 'NO'

THE KING, THE "DAILY MIRROR" UNDERSTANDS, HAS TOLD THE CABINET OF HIS WISH TO MARRY MRS. SIMPSON, AMERICAN-BORN SOCIETY WOMAN NOW LIVING IN LONDON. THE CABINET HAS ADVISED AGAINST IT.

LAST NIGHT THE KING AND THE PRIME MINISTER DISCUSSED THE MATTER AT BUCKINGHAM PALACE FOR ONE HOUR AND FORTY MINUTES. EARLIER IN THE DAY THE CABINET HAD SAT FOR TWO AND A HALF HOURS SEEKING A WAY OUT OF THEIR DIFFICULTY.

MR. BALDWIN LEFT THE HOUSE OF COMMONS HURRIEDLY IN THE MIDDLE OF A DEBATE TO DRIVE BY CAR TO THE PALACE.

On arrival there at ten minutes to six he was immediately received by the King. It was not until half-past seven that, looking intensely serious and smoking his pipe, he drove away again.

This was the second audience Mr. Baldwin has had with the King within a week.

Twenty minutes after Mr. Baldwin had gone King Edward left Buckingham Palace by car alone.

Yesterday was a day of grave discussions in Whitehall and uncertainty in the City.

NOT EUROPE

SHARP DROP IN GOVERNMENT STOCKS

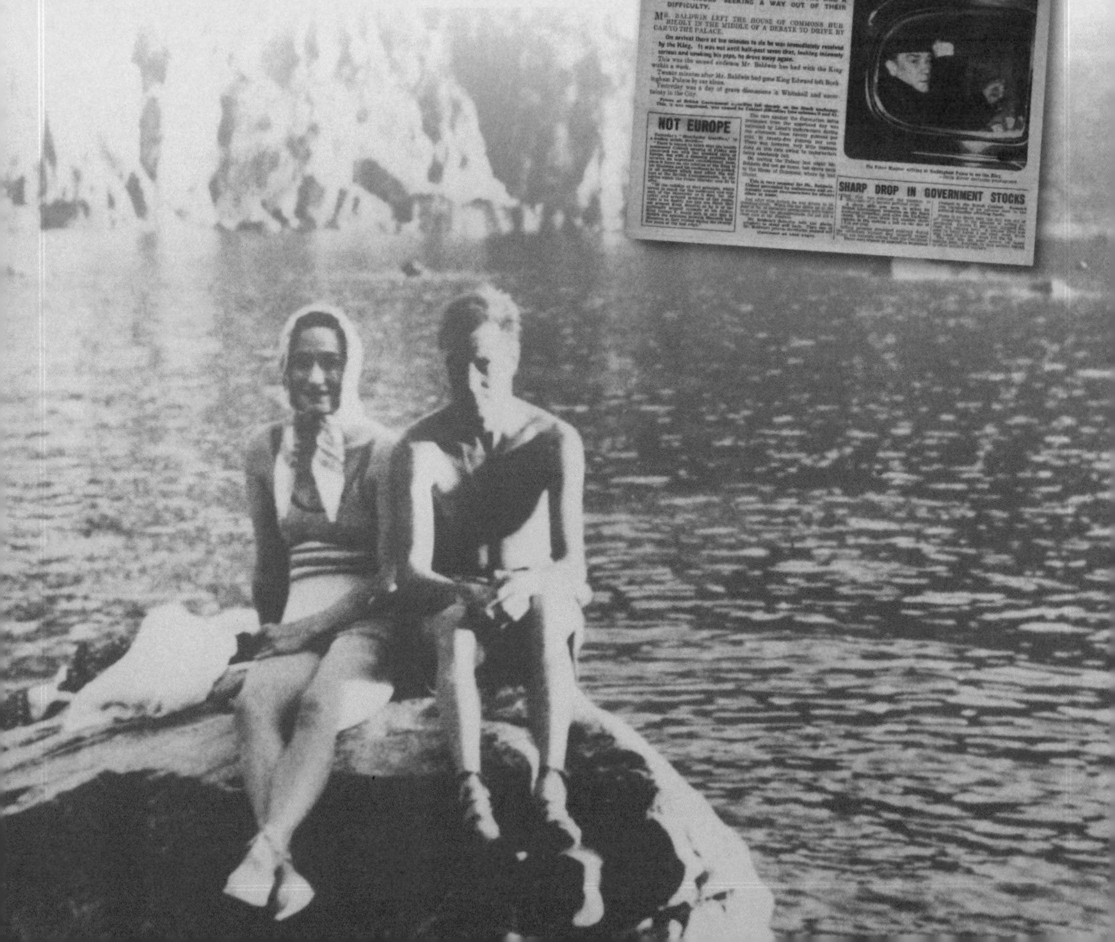

as their queen. Edward proposed they have a morganatic marriage in which Wallis did not become queen but was given some lesser title instead. This was rejected by Parliament and by the heads of countries around the Empire. Edward could have married against the will of his ministers, but he knew the government would then have resigned, causing a constitutional crisis.

In the midst of the furor, Wallis fled across the Channel to France, terrified that she would be assassinated. By telephone she urged Edward not to resign. This wasn't what she wanted at all. She was quite happy being a King's mistress, with all the attendant perks, and knew that if he abdicated because of her she would be vilified by press and public

RIGHT
Married at last, June 3, 1937, at the cost to Edward of his country and his crown. Her blue dress was designed by Mainbocher to match the exact shade of her eyes.

alike. However, on December 10, Edward
told his brother Albert that he was stepping
down, and the negotiation over terms
began. He wrote in his memoirs that as
soon as he had made the decision he felt

*Wallis fled, terrified she
would be assassinated*

marvelous, "like a swimmer surfacing from
a great depth." The news was broadcast on the BBC that evening and
Edward left Britain for Austria. American ironist H.L. Mencken called
it "the greatest news story since the Resurrection."

It was four months before Edward and Wallis could meet again,
as her divorce from Ernest was going through on grounds of his
infidelity and could founder if there were charges of collusion. She
was a nervous wreck as the house where she was staying was staked
out by journalists and every postal delivery brought more sacks of
hate mail and death threats. In May 1937, she was at last able to join
Edward, now styled the Duke of Windsor, and on June 3, they
married in a château near Tours. She became the Duchess of
Windsor, but to the fury of both was refused the title "Her Royal
Highness." They were also upset that they would not receive income
from the civil list but would be given an allowance by Edward's
brother, the new king George VI. What's more, this allowance
could be revoked if Edward returned to Britain without an invitation.
Wallis and Edward were officially in exile and relations between him
and his family remained tense for decades afterward.

It wasn't long before they found themselves in more trouble. Both
had expressed support for Fascism as a bulwark against Communism,
but their decision to meet Adolf Hitler
in October 1937 handed the Germans
a stunning propaganda coup. When the
Second World War began, they were living
in France, and there were claims that
Edward had leaked some important details
about Britain's plans for the defense
of Belgium to the Germans. Rumors
spread that Hitler might kidnap them
and attempt to put Edward back on the
throne, especially after he commented that
Wallis would have made a good queen.
There was also a rumor that Wallis had
had an affair with the German ambassador,

BELOW
*The ill-judged, high-profile
meeting with Adolf Hitler in
October 1937. According to
Edward, "His eyes were
piercing and magnetic. I
confess frankly that he took
me in. I believed him when
he implied that he sought
no war with England."*

"You have no idea how hard it is to live out a great romance"

von Ribbentrop, in London back in 1936. The Windsors were clearly a liability so in August 1940, Prime Minister Winston Churchill ordered them to sail for the Bahamas, where Edward was to be governor, a post he hated.

After the war, they returned to France. Edward had no official role any more, so theirs was a life of parties and café society, of high fashion and extravagance. They sailed back and forth to America (Wallis was afraid of flying), always taking their pug dogs with them, and met movie stars and presidents, twice being invited to dinner at the White House. The relationship was often strained, though, and there was never any question who was boss, as Wallis barked orders at her husband in full hearing of those present.

"You have no idea how hard it is to live out a great romance," she remarked later in life. None of it had turned out the way the fiercely ambitious Wallis had planned. Instead of gaining power and influence through her affair with Edward, they became self-indulgent socialites with nothing to do except shop and travel. Instead of gaining acceptance in high society, Wallis became a pariah. It was a harsh twist of fate.

Edward died of throat cancer in 1972 and Queen Elizabeth II invited Wallis to stay in Buckingham Palace and attend the funeral at St. George's Chapel in the grounds of Windsor Castle. Thereafter, Wallis became a recluse at her home in Paris, seeing few people apart from her French lawyer Suzanne Blum, who took over her affairs and, some say, exploited her wealth for personal gain. Her funeral in 1986 was also held in Windsor Castle where she was buried next to Edward in the royal burial ground. The British royal family finally allowed them to return to the fold—but only once they could no longer cause any trouble.

ABDICATION

Throughout history, rulers have abdicated for different reasons. Roman emperor Diocletian voluntarily gave up power in 305 CE after twenty years in charge, and retired to a luxurious villa in Split. Charles V, the Hapsburg monarch, who ruled Spain, Austria, the Netherlands, and most of Latin America, stepped aside in 1556 after 37 years on the throne. Others have been forced to abdicate: Richard II had to do so after Henry Bolingbroke seized power; Mary, Queen of Scots, was made to step down in favor of her one-year-old son; James II of England and VII of Scotland was deemed to have abdicated when he fled the country in the wake of the Glorious Revolution; and Tsar Nicholas II had to abdicate during the Russian Revolution. But Edward VIII's abdication caused shockwaves because it was both voluntary and right at the beginning of his reign. Throughout history those born into royal families had accepted they could not marry freely, but Edward claimed, "I have found it impossible to carry the heavy burden of . . . my duties . . . without the help and support of the woman I love."

INSTRUMENT OF ABDICATION

I, Edward the Eighth, of Great Britain, Ireland, and the British Dominions beyond the Seas, King, Emperor of India, do hereby declare My irrevocable determination to renounce the Throne for Myself and for My descendants, and My desire that effect should be given to this Instrument of Abdication immediately.

In token whereof I have hereunto set My hand this tenth day of December, nineteen hundred and thirty six, in the presence of the witnesses whose signatures are subscribed.

Edward RI

SIGNED AT
FORT BELVEDERE
IN THE PRESENCE
OF

Albert

Henry

George

LEFT
The formal document with which Edward irrevocably gave up his throne on December 10, 1936.

Prince Bertil of Sweden
– & –
Lilian Craig

Bertil Gustaf Oskar Carl Eugén
Born: February 28, 1912, Stockholm, Sweden
Died: January 5, 1997, Djurgården, Sweden

Lillian May Davies
Born: August 30, 1915, Swansea, Wales
Died: March 10, 2013, Stockholm, Sweden

Married December 7, 1976

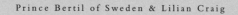

Bertil knew Lilian was married so didn't try to pursue her romantically——but there was definitely a mutual attraction from the start

It was the height of the Second World War when Lilian first caught Bertil's eye in a crowded London nightclub. He introduced himself as the Prince of Sweden, and she threw her head back and laughed, replying, "How wonderful! I'm the Queen of Sheba."

*L*ooking at her family background, no one could possibly have predicted that young Lillian Davies would ever have anything to do with royalty. Her father, William, ran a market stall in Swansea, South Wales, and worked in a factory that made charcoal briquettes, while her mother, Mary, was a shop assistant. Both came from decent working-class families who wanted to avoid scandal, so when Mary became pregnant there was a hasty wedding four months before the baby was due. Her parents' was not a happy marriage, though, and when Lillian was still very young, her father left and money became particularly tight. Lillian left school at the age of fourteen to take a job in a shop and contribute to the family income: "We were very poor and had to work hard," she recalled in her memoirs. "There was no joy, no life . . . nothing."

Lillian was a stunningly beautiful girl with a zest for life and the depressed mining port town of Swansea was never going to be enough for her. In 1933, when she turned eighteen, she headed for the bright lights of London, where she dreamed of becoming an actress and a singer. Her big break came when she was spotted by a model agent and began to get jobs in advertising and magazines, including a shoot for *Vogue*, despite the fact that she was much more petite than the usual fashion model. She also got bit parts in a few movies, and began to receive invitations to glitzy parties and social events. It was around this time that she dropped the second "l" in her name, deciding that "Lilian" had a classier look.

Just after the Second World War began, she met Ivan Craig, a Scottish actor from a wealthy family. He had already signed up to fight, so they got married quickly before he was shipped out to North Africa. Lilian later described it as "a typical wartime marriage," as they hadn't known each other for long before the wedding and would live separate lives for the duration of the war. She stayed in her husband's

OPPOSITE
Lilian and Bertil had different memories of their first meeting: he thought it was at her 28th birthday party, while she was positive it was in a nightclub.

Knightsbridge apartment, and took a job in a factory that made radio sets for the navy, also volunteering at a hospital in East Grinstead.

The German bombing raids that began in 1940 were utterly terrifying for Londoners, but the nightlife continued for those brave enough to risk stepping out. One night in August 1943, Lilian went with friends to a fashionable club called Les Ambassadeurs, where she met the very attractive Prince Bertil. She liked him right away and invited him to a small party she was throwing for her birthday on August 30, a few days later. He arrived carrying a white orchid as a gift, and they spent much of the evening chatting. Bertil knew Lilian was married so didn't try to pursue her romantically, but they stayed in touch. It seems there was definitely a mutual attraction from the start.

A DUTIFUL SON

As the third son of Crown Prince Gustav Adolf and his first wife, British-born Princess Margaret, Prince Bertil shouldn't have had to worry about the succession to the Swedish throne. His grandfather was the reigning monarch while he was a boy, making Bertil fourth in line behind his father and older brothers. He also had a sister, Ingrid, and a younger brother, Prince Carl Johan, who was born in 1916. Their mother tragically died four years later during her sixth pregnancy. Bertil was taught in the palace in Stockholm until the age of twelve, then sent to the city's Beskow School where he could be educated alongside non-royal children in a move that was considered progressive

BELOW
The Swedish royal children (from left to right): Princess Ingrid, Prince Gustaf Adolf, Prince Bertil, and Prince Sigvard. On the right is a photo of Princess Margaret with Bertil and Ingrid.

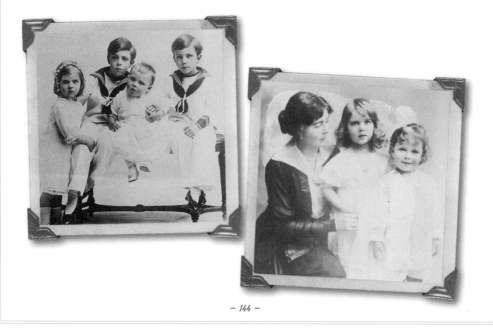

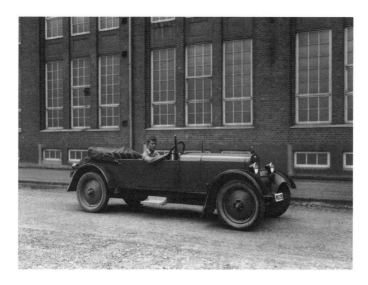

LEFT
*Bertil at the wheel of a
Thulin B automobile in
1928. Only thirteen of
these cars were ever built.*

at the time. He suffered from dyslexia and didn't do well in his studies,
but developed a lifelong passion for sports. After school, he enrolled
in the navy and began to undertake royal duties—as well as squiring
a succession of beautiful young women around town.

In 1934, Bertil fell in love with a girl called Margareta Brambeck
and asked his grandfather's permission to marry her. The answer that
came back was a resounding "no." According to the 1810 Act of
Succession, Swedish royals were only allowed to marry other royals,
and to do otherwise would mean forfeiting their place in the line
of succession. Sigvard, one of Bertil's older brothers, had done just
that when he married a commoner in March 1934, meaning that
Bertil was now third in line to the throne after his father and older
brother, also called Gustav Adolf. The royal house couldn't afford to
lose another heir, so Bertil was dispatched to Paris as an assistant naval
attaché and instructed to forget all about Miss Brambeck. While there,
he comforted himself with a string of glamorous French girls, and also
developed a taste for fast automobiles, gourmet food, and good living.

After war broke out in 1939, Sweden announced its neutrality
and in August 1942 Bertil was posted to London as an assistant naval
attaché, to observe and advise his country on British naval matters that
might affect Sweden. It was there in 1943 that he met the glamorous
Lilian Craig. Her husband had finished his service in North Africa
but was now fighting his way up through Italy with the British Army,
having been promoted to the rank of major. Lilian rarely saw him,

MONARCHIES IN WARTIME

During World War II, the monarchs of neutral countries such as Sweden and Spain could remain on their thrones, but those in countries invaded by the Nazis either had to flee or to work with the invaders. In May 1940, King Haakon of Norway escaped on a British cruiser after refusing to accept a Nazi puppet government, and he went to London to lead resistance to his country's occupation while his wife and family went to the US. Queen Wilhelmina and Prince Bernhard of the Netherlands also made a base in London where they worked with the Dutch government in exile. There they were caught up in the Blitz, as Germany bombed the British capital, but survived the war to take the throne again in 1945. King George II of Greece evacuated most of his family to South Africa. Christian X of Denmark stayed on the throne throughout the Nazi occupation and helped the country's Jewish people to escape across the border into Sweden. But some monarchs who remained on the throne, including Leopold III of Belgium and Prince Louis II of Monaco, were criticized for working a little too closely with the occupying forces.

and Bertil felt instinctively protective of her. One night in 1943, while he was dining at the Dorchester Hotel with a group that included Princess Marina of Great Britain, the widow of the Duke of Kent, Bertil heard that there had been bombing in Knightsbridge near Lilian's home. He immediately left the table to telephone from the lobby and see if she was all right. She said that she was but the area was being evacuated, and she sounded so scared that Bertil instantly said he would come and fetch her. He drove through the streets of the capital in the aftermath of the bombing raid, dressed in a dinner jacket, with debris still falling from buildings. Lilian's road was closed because of an unexploded bomb, but Bertil gallantly managed to get through and rescue her. There was no chance of finding her a room in a hotel that night, so he instructed his Hungarian cook to make up a guest bedroom at his apartment in Edwardes Square, Kensington. According to Lilian's memoirs, "We were not a couple when I moved in. But we soon

became one." The attraction between them was just too great to withstand. "He was so handsome, my prince," she wrote. "So charming and thoughtful. And so funny. Oh, how we laughed together."

"He was so handsome, my prince"

They were lovers for the remainder of the war, then in May 1945 Bertil was asked by his grandfather to become a trade ambassador for Sweden, traveling the world to promote Swedish industry. It was a role that suited the genial, extrovert prince to a tee, although it made it more difficult for him to see Lilian since he no longer had an official base in London. Worse still, Ivan Craig had returned from the fighting and although he and Lilian had lost contact during the war and he admitted to having fallen in love with an Italian woman, he was at first reluctant to agree to a divorce, hoping to rekindle the relationship and thus avoid scandal. Prince Bertil met him in the Ritz Hotel for a man-to-man discussion, and eventually Ivan agreed to give Lilian a divorce after making Bertil promise that he would always look after her. The three would remain friends for life.

There still remained the problem of the succession to the Swedish throne, but this was simplifed in April 1946 when a son was born to Bertil's oldest brother, Prince Gustaf Adolf. Thus the boy took Bertil's place as third in line, and it seemed the globetrotting prince was going to be let off the hook. But nine months later, Prince Gustaf Adolf was tragically killed in a plane crash over Denmark and Bertil's role in the dynasty instantly became crucial. His grandfather was eighty-eight, his father was sixty-four, and his nephew was just an infant. It seemed likely that the child, Prince Carl Gustaf, would succeed to the throne before reaching the age of majority, in which case a regent would be necessary. Bertil's younger brother Prince Carl Johan had by this time married a commoner, so as the succession act decreed, Bertil was the only remaining family member who could fulfill the role. But if he married Lilian, a commoner and a divorcee to boot, he would no longer be eligible to help. "My father demanded that I think of Sweden first and I understood that he was right," Bertil told his

OPPOSITE
While serving as a naval attaché in London, Bertil made his way around on a motorcycle. He often socialized with the British royal family during the war years.

biographer later in life. "[My father and I] were both in trouble and
had no other choice. I felt devastated. It was one of the darkest days
of my life."

Bertil could have followed his brothers' example and stepped out
of the line of succession, but instead, for the time being, he chose to
put duty ahead of love. He would be the loyal son, the one who put
his royal responsibilities above the promptings of his heart. But still
he couldn't give up Lilian. He asked her to wait for him until the
succession was secured, and she was so completely and utterly in love
with him that she agreed.

A WAIT THAT LASTED THREE DECADES

Lilian visited Sweden for the first time in 1946 and stayed with close
friends of Prince Bertil's in a borrowed apartment. He then bought
a house, Villa Solbacken, in Djurgården, a fashionable district of the
city, to make it easier for them to be together, but they couldn't dine
openly in restaurants or socialize except with a close-knit circle of
people he trusted. He also bought a holiday home at Sainte-Maxime
on the French Riviera, then a reasonably quiet resort where they
were able to live freely without fear of recognition. They had a lively
social life in France with members of the international jet-set, all of
them sworn to secrecy, and enjoyed playing golf together and riding
on Bertil's motorcycle or in one of his fast cars. Lilian was not
introduced to the Swedish royal family, and Bertil asked the Swedish
press, with whom he was on excellent terms, to agree not to write

about them, in return for which he promised he
would share the full story when the time was right.

At first, Lilian commuted between London,
Stockholm, and Sainte-Maxime, but in 1957 she
moved to Stockholm to live full-time with Bertil.
By then his family had found out about their
relationship. At first his sister Ingrid and sister-in-law
Sibylla were convinced that Lilian was a fortune
hunter, but they soon learned to appreciate her
loyalty to Bertil. His father, who had succeeded to
the throne in 1950, found her warm and charming.
He wouldn't consent to their marriage, but he began
to invite Lilian to family events. She was present
at King Gustav Adolf's eightieth birthday party in
1962, but declined to attend Princess Desirée's
wedding in 1964. "I would only have been able
to go to church and would have had to go home
afterwards when the rest of the family went to lunch
at the Royal Palace," she explained. "So I watched
everything on TV instead." It was often lonely for
her when Bertil went off to fulfill royal duties and
she stayed home alone, but it was a price she was
willing to pay to be with him. There was one more
great sacrifice they made, something they would
both regret: they did not have any children. For
Bertil, having a live-in mistress was one thing, but
illegitimate children would have been a step too far.

In 1971, Prince Carl Gustaf turned twenty-five,
the age at which he was eligible to reign, but still
Bertil's father asked him to refrain from marrying
Lilian until the Prince had married and the
succession was assured. In a growing sign of her
acceptance by the family, Lilian was invited to attend
the King's ninetieth birthday celebrations in 1972
and then his funeral in 1973. Bertil helped his
nephew take up the reins of power and accompanied
him as regent on overseas trips. When King Carl
Gustaf introduced Bertil to his girlfriend, Silvia
Sommerlath, Bertil's reaction was immediate: "Marry
her!" he cried—and they did just that, in June 1976.

ROYALTY ON THE RIVIERA

The Grimaldi royal family have
been based in Monaco for
centuries, but it was only in
the late 19th century that other
European royals began to
discover the beauty of France's
south coast. Queen Victoria of
Great Britain arrived in Nice in
1882 and was instantly smitten
by what she called "the sunny,
flowery south." She began to
spend so much time there that
her ministers back home became
alarmed. Word spread, and the
wealthy elite flocked to the area.
Leopold II of Belgium bought up
the land around Cap Ferrat and
developed it into a playground
for the rich. Other royals arrived,
including Nicholas II of Russia
and Duleep Singh, last Maharajah
of the Sikh Empire. In the early
years of the 20th century,
actors and writers—among
them, Charlie Chaplin, F. Scott
Fitzgerald, and W. Somerset
Maugham—popularized the
Riviera but it remained a place
where royalty could still expect
to enjoy privacy. Indeed, Wallis
Simpson hid there during the
abdication crisis (see page 136)
and in the 1950s and 60s it
was still exclusive enough for
Prince Bertil and Lilian Craig to
dine in local restaurants without
fear of discovery.

The succession was finally secured, and at last the way was clear for Bertil and Lilian to marry. Their wedding was planned for the following December, more than thirty-three years after their first meeting; he was sixty-four, she sixty-one.

Before the wedding, Lilian had to take Swedish nationality; they were then married in the tiny chapel at Drottningholm Palace in Stockholm on December 7, 1976. She wore an ice-blue gown and carried a bouquet of lilies-of-the-valley. After placing the ring on her finger, Bertil kissed his new bride's hand. King Carl Gustaf ordained that despite marrying a "commoner," Bertil could keep all his titles and his place in the succession so that he could always be called upon to help out as regent if necessary. It meant that Lilian was now Her Royal Highness Princess Lilian, Duchess of Halland. "It feels wonderful to become a Swedish princess and feel recognized after all these years," she told a packed press conference when their "secret" was announced to the nation.

BELOW
Lilian and Bertil finally marry in December 1976. She admitted afterward, "I was nervous as a kitten. I had butterflies in my stomach. When we exchanged vows, I was afraid I wouldn't even remember my husband's name."

Lilian embraced royal duties after her marriage and proved to be adept at meeting and greeting foreign dignitaries. She was good at putting people at ease, especially with her fondness for practical jokes—she once tricked President Ronald Reagan with a fake ketchup bottle. She proved very popular with the Swedish people, and became close friends with

ABOVE
The 1976 Nobel Prize ceremony on December 10, attended by two sets of royal newlyweds: Queen Silvia and King Carl Gustaf flanked by Prince Bertil and Lilian.

Queen Silvia and a loving surrogate grandmother to the royal children. At last she could accompany Bertil on overseas trips, and they particularly enjoyed representing Sweden at the Olympic Games and attending the annual Nobel Prize ceremonies.

Just a month after their twentieth wedding anniversary, in January 1997, Bertil died after a short illness, with Lilian holding his hand. As Lilian struggled with her overwhelming grief, Queen Silvia came to sleep on a cot in her room to keep her company. The family bought her a yellow Labrador she called Bingo, who became her faithful companion at that difficult time. She continued to be a working royal until after her ninetieth birthday, and was a strong supporter of the charity SOS Children's Villages, which provides accommodation for children whose biological families are unable to care for them. Following Lilian's death in 2013, at the age of 98, she was laid to rest with her beloved Prince in the beautiful royal burial ground at Haga in Solna, just outside Stockholm. No laws or family obligations could separate them again.

It was an unconventional relationship for many years and it must have been difficult for both of them, but there was never any question of giving up because their bond was too strong. "If I were to sum up my life, everything has been about my love," Lilian explained to her husband's biographer in 1995. "He's a great man, and I love him."

> "*If I were to sum up my life, everything has been about my love*"

Prince Rainier III & Princess Grace
of Monaco

Prince Rainier III
– & –
Grace Kelly

Rainier Louis Henri Maxence Bertrand Grimaldi
Born: May 31, 1923, Monaco Died: April 6, 2005, Monaco

Grace Patricia Kelly
Born: November 12, 1929, Philadelphia, U.S. Died: September 14, 1982, Monaco

Married April 18, 1956

ABOVE
Playboy Rainier in 1954. He said in an interview that his greatest difficulty was "knowing a girl long enough and intimately enough to find out if [they] were soul mates as well as lovers."

RIGHT
Grace in 1955 with her Best Actress Oscar for The Country Girl. *She cried during her brief acceptance speech, telling reporters later, "I was just happy because it meant that now I too belonged to the family."*

"He liked skiing, motor racing, stalking wild boar—and wining and dining pretty women"

Prince Rainier had a list of qualities he wanted in a wife: she must have been raised a Catholic, she should be intelligent, pretty and charming, she should come from a wealthy family—and she must be fertile. Grace Kelly seemed tailor-made for the role.

R ainier was born into the House of Grimaldi, which had ruled the tiny principality of Monaco in the South of France since 1297. From childhood, his role was made clear to him: he would one day preside over the country and be responsible for the welfare of its citizens, and he must marry and produce an heir. If he didn't, under a 1918 treaty with France, Monaco would revert to French rule. He knew this from a young age, long before his parents divorced when he was six years old and his father sent him to Summerfields prep school in St. Leonards-on-Sea in southern England. From there he went to Stowe public school in Buckinghamshire, where he was bullied by the other boys for being both Catholic and foreign. He became a loner and learned how to put on a brave face to hide his feelings. At fourteen, he was sent to school in Geneva, and in 1944 he graduated from the respected École Libre des Sciences Politiques in Paris.

When he returned to Monaco, Rainier fell out with his grandfather, the country's sovereign, over the latter's implicit support for the German occupation of France. Rainier rebelled by joining the Free French forces and fought the Germans at Alsace, winning a Croix de Guerre and a Bronze Star for his valor in battle. After the war, he headed for Berlin to work for a French military mission, and began to gain a reputation for fast living. He liked skiing, motor racing, stalking wild boar—and wining and dining pretty women. Then in 1949, on the death of his grandfather, he became ruler of Monaco, since his mother had renounced her rights to the throne in his favor.

Rainier took over a country that was teetering on the verge of bankruptcy. The pre-war economy had been based on Europe's wealthy aristocrats coming to gamble at the casino, and business had been badly

BELOW
Rainier wearing his medals and decorations for a formal state occasion in 1954. His wartime awards included a French and a Belgian Croix de Guerre, an Italian Merit Cross, and a Lebanese Medal of Merit.

damaged by the war. Rainier needed a fresh approach, and he decided to turn Monaco into a tax haven, to encourage commercial development and to revitalize tourism. Choosing the right wife would help. He had a long-term girlfriend, Frenchwoman Gisèle Pascal, but when his doctors tested her they deemed her infertile, which ruled her out as a potential mate. Unknown to Rainier, one of his advisors had approached Marilyn Monroe and asked if she might be interested in the role. She wasn't Catholic and had been married before, so she was unsuitable on many levels; fortunately, she declined. And then in May 1955, a *Paris-Match* correspondent set up a meeting between Rainier and Hollywood actress Grace Kelly, while she was in the South of France filming *To Catch A Thief*. It was intended purely as a publicity stunt for the magazine, but a spark was kindled that would lead to the Philadelphia-born actress giving up the life she knew and taking a leap into the unknown . . .

THE WORLD'S MOST ELIGIBLE BACHELOR

BELOW
Grace attended a prestigious Catholic girls' school. In the "prophecy" section of her graduation yearbook, it read, "Miss Grace P. Kelly—a famous star of stage and screen."

Grace Kelly was the third of four children born to John Kelly, owner of a thriving building company and a man who had won two Olympic gold medals for sculling. The family was very athletic and competitive and Grace, an imaginative, feminine child, was the odd one out with her love of dressing up dolls and playing make-believe. She discovered a talent for acting in her early teens, taking on many roles at Philadelphia's Academy Players, and she also found that she was popular with boys. "Men began proposing to my daughter Grace when she was barely fifteen," her mother said in a later interview. There was one serious boyfriend while she was still at school, then many more when she went to study at the American Academy of Dramatic Arts in New York. She lived in a women-only hotel, and dressed sedately in white gloves, tailored suits and flat shoes, but had soon begun an affair with one of her college tutors, Don Richardson, which drove her parents to distraction. The Kellys were social climbers and Don did not fit any of the criteria they wanted in a husband for their daughter.

GRACE KELLY, STYLE ICON

In an era when Hollywood's leading ladies tended to wear skin-tight gowns with plunging necklines, accessorized with tottering heels and lots of jewelry, Grace Kelly opted for a simple, classic style. For daywear, she favored Capri pants with crisp cotton shirts, flat shoes, and tortoiseshell sunglasses, and for evening she'd wear dresses in candy colors with fitted waists and modest scoop necks. Before meeting Prince Rainier, Grace dated designer Oleg Cassini and wore some of his evening gowns for big occasions, such as the Cannes Film Festival in 1954. Top movie fashion designer Edith Head made the green silk draped dress with a bustle that she wore to collect her Best Actress Oscar in 1955, and MGM's designer Helen Rose made her magnificent vintage lace wedding gown with its high neckline and buttoned sleeves. As Princess Grace, she patronized the top designers in Paris—Dior, Balenciaga, Saint-Laurent and Givenchy—without compromising the simplicity of her look. When she carried a large Hermès bag to hide her pregnancy bump, the company were so delighted that they designed a bag that would be named the Kelly bag in her honor.

ABOVE
Grace did some modeling when starting out, including a commercial in which she had to spray insecticide, but she wasn't considered thin enough for high fashion work.

Grace worked as a model and television actress before moving into movies. Her first movie role was as Gary Cooper's Quaker wife in *High Noon*, for which John Ford hired her after a screen test that he said showed "breeding, quality and style." She followed that with a co-starring role in *Mogambo*, with Clark Gable and Ava Gardner, for which she won a Golden Globe as Best Supporting Actress. But it was when she was discovered by Oscar-winning director Alfred Hitchcock, who cast her in leading roles in *Dial M for Murder* and *Rear Window*, that Grace became a star. Her glacial blonde beauty carried a strong appeal for cinema audiences and, even though she didn't have much range as an actress, by the end of 1954 she was the biggest star in Hollywood alongside Marilyn Monroe. In *The Country Girl*, as the wife of a washed-up alcoholic singer, played by Bing Crosby, she earned the top prize Hollywood had to offer: an Oscar at the 1955 Academy Awards. Her screen image was that of a pure, virginal type but Hollywood gossip columnists linked her with a number of her co-stars, including Bing Crosby, William Holden, and Ray Milland. According to her sister Lizanne, "There was something about her that men just went ape about," but the men she was dating

BELOW
Cary Grant and Grace Kelly in To Catch a Thief *(1955). He said of his co-star, "Grace acted the way Johnny Weissmuller swam, or Fred Astaire danced. She made it look easy."*

were older than her, they were either married or divorced, and her parents disapproved. Then, on May 6, 1955, at the age of twenty-five, Grace went to the palace in Monaco at the instigation of *Paris-Match* and met Rainier, then the world's most eligible bachelor.

Grace and Rainier shook hands and he offered to show her around his private zoo. She was impressed when he reached through the bars of the cage to pet a tiger and they chatted easily—except when they had to stop and pose for the photographers who were trailing behind them. When asked afterwards what she thought of him, Grace said, "He is charming, so very charming." Rainier later said that he made up his mind almost straightaway to ask for her hand in marriage. He asked one of his advisors, Father Tucker, to write to Grace and test the waters, and she responded positively, after which she and Rainier began to correspond and to telephone each other. Father Tucker reported that Rainier was "all aglow" and "full of little exuberances." Grace was working in America and he was tied down with state business in Monaco, but they became closer and closer during the remainder of 1955 and he asked if he might come over to visit her family over Christmas. She agreed, and during the Christmas holiday they became engaged.

Grace's parents were delighted—what better match could they have wished for? They were slightly less enamored when Rainier's lawyers arrived to negotiate the marriage contract and intimated that they expected her father to pay a hefty dowry (said to be around two million dollars). Grace had to endure a medical exam to prove her fertility and then the deal was struck. "Oh my God, Grace, you don't even know this guy," her sister Lizanne protested, but Grace later explained, simply, "When I was with him, I was happy wherever we were." She was leaving Hollywood at the pinnacle of her career, having just won an Oscar, but she knew that fewer roles would be offered as she got older and, besides, she had always wanted to marry well and have children. It seemed as though Rainier had come along at exactly the right time.

"*When I was with him, I was happy wherever we were*"

ABOVE
Grace's first meeting with Rainier in May 1955. The outfit she wanted to wear was creased and a power outage prevented her from ironing it, so she had to choose this loud-patterned dress with red and green roses on a black satin background.

ABOVE
Grace Kelly photographed in her wedding dress, holding her bouquet of lily-of-the-valley. "It was a nightmare, really, the whole thing," she said years later.

WEDDING OF THE CENTURY

The media went into a frenzy when the marriage was announced, and grew more and more excited as the big day approached. Grace bought her trousseau from New York's top designers and set sail for Monaco on the *SS Constitution*, along with seventy-two friends and relatives— and the world's press, who expected press conferences and photo calls every day of the voyage. The people of Monaco lined the shores to cheer as Rainier's yacht sailed out to bring her ashore, and from then on the wedding became a media junket, with 1,500 journalists packed into the tiny principality. Grace lost ten pounds in weight with the stress of the expectations heaped upon her and was exhausted as she sat through the long, pompous civil ceremony on April 18, 1956, followed by a church wedding the following day. Guests included Aristotle Onassis, Gloria Swanson, Ava Gardner, David Niven, and the Aga Khan. She was relieved when they set sail on Rainier's yacht for a honeymoon around the coasts of France and Spain, giving her a chance to relax and get to know the new husband with whom she had so far spent very little time.

On their return to Monaco, Rainier went straight back to work, leaving Grace alone in his bachelor apartment with nothing to do. She spent her days writing letters and telephoning friends back home, and she soon became terribly homesick. There were hundreds of staff members but no one to talk to, and Rainier could be moody and dictatorial when affairs of state were fraught. Within six weeks, Grace had fulfilled part of her side of the bargain by becoming pregnant but she suffered badly from morning sickness and put on a lot of weight, which she hated. In January 1957, a daughter they named Caroline was born, then the following year she gave birth to a son and heir for

Rainier, named Albert. The Prince was overjoyed and showered
Grace with presents of diamonds and orchids. She threw herself
wholeheartedly into motherhood, speaking out as an advocate of
breastfeeding at a time when formula was gaining in popularity.
The couple bought a farmhouse, Roc Agel, where they could relax
and lead a simple life far removed from the pomp and ceremony of
royal life in Monaco. Gradually, Grace and Rainier began to fall in
love with each other.

As well as being a devoted mother, Grace involved herself
in charity work in the community. She raised funds for the hospital
and a center for the elderly, held an annual gala to raise money
for the Red Cross, and started the Princess Grace Foundation to
sponsor the arts. Rainier had some tricky political problems to solve
when his modernization plans were blocked by the National Council.
Although he was head of state, he shared power with the Council
and, after they bogged down his 1959 budget in red tape, he
suspended them. It was a time of tense stand-off, but in 1962
Rainier brought in a new, modernized, democratically
elected National Council, at the same time significantly
reducing his own power, although his signature was still
required on proposed laws. He also ran into trouble with
the French government, who objected to Monaco's
tax-free status, which was attracting French businesses to
relocate there. French customs officials blocked the roads in
and out of the principality and for a while its independence

BELOW
*Grace and Rainier with
their children Albert and
Caroline at Albert's baptism
(bottom); and an image of
Grace and baby Albert on
a 1958 stamp. "I am not
going to let public life or
anything else drive me out
of my role as a mother,"
Grace insisted.*

was threatened. Rainier was forced to agree a compromise in which only businesses that had been established in Monaco for five years could remain tax-free, and the crisis blew over. Grace's glamor attracted new visitors, and tourist revenues improved dramatically.

Grace hoped for more children but had two miscarriages before giving birth to a daughter, Stéphanie, in 1965. Shortly afterward, she was back in America for her father's funeral when she heard rumors that Rainier was having an affair with one of her ladies-in-waiting. He denied it point blank, but on her return Grace fired the lady in question. It wasn't the last time such gossip would emerge—there would later be gossip of Rainier's "Paris ladies"—but it wasn't the biggest problem in their marriage. Grace's lack of fulfillment was perhaps more damaging. She missed acting terribly. Occasionally, parts were still offered, but Rainier always deemed them inappropriate for someone in her position. In 1962 when Hitchcock offered her the lead role in his film *Marnie*, at last her husband agreed she could take it, but when it was announced publicly there was such an outcry in Monaco that she had to back down. The people didn't want their Princess abandoning them for Hollywood. Sadly, she gave up the idea. When Rainier asked her what she would like as a present for their tenth wedding anniversary in 1966, she replied, "A year off!"

BELOW
Grace and Rainier with Albert, Caroline, and Stéphanie. Grace was a strict mother who once bit Caroline's arm to show her what it felt like so she would stop biting other children.

TRAGEDY ON THE CORNICHE

During the late 1970s, Grace began giving poetry readings, and found it satisfied some of her creative urges. She also loved making intricate dried-flower collages. She was distressed by her daughter Caroline's

"They had little in common, but there was genuine love"

affair with and subsequent marriage to a playboy called Philippe Junot, who was wildly unfaithful, and according to friends Grace was turning more often to alcohol. She'd always enjoyed a stiff cocktail but now she drank more and began to gain weight. She and Rainier argued frequently and led lives that were often quite separate. Then on the morning of September 13, 1982, she got into her car with Stéphanie to drive from Roc Agel to Monaco with some clothes she was taking to her couturier for alterations. The steep, twisting road known as the Corniche had more than fifty sharp turns and, to the horror of a driver just behind them, Grace's car swerved then failed to make one of the turns, hurtling over a precipice and landing on its roof. Stéphanie managed to crawl out of the wreck, injured, and raise the alarm, but Grace never regained consciousness. It appears she had suffered a brain hemorrhage, which may have caused the accident, and she died the following day.

Rainier was so distraught that he even considered abdicating the throne. World dignitaries, including Princess Diana, Cary Grant, and Nancy Reagan, came to Monaco for the funeral, at which Rainier was supported by his shocked and grief-stricken children. He and Grace had survived many crises during their marriage, and on paper they had little in common. They certainly hadn't known each other well before they wed. Grace wrote toward the end of her life that Catholicism was the mutual bond that kept their marriage together, but, from Rainier's reaction to her death, it seems there was genuine love as well. He lived for another twenty-three years but never remarried.

THE CURSE OF THE GRIMALDIS

According to legend, a medieval sorceress put a curse on the House of Grimaldi, vowing, "No Grimaldi will ever find happiness in marriage," after Prince Rainier I kidnapped and raped a beautiful young maiden in the 13th century. True to form, Rainier's parents divorced and fought a bitter court battle for custody of him in 1929. It seemed the family's luck had changed when Rainier wed Grace, but then came the disastrous car crash and her death at the age of just fifty-two. Each of their three children has suffered marital woes. Caroline's first marriage to Philippe Junot was annulled and then, just when it seemed she had found happiness with Italian businessman Stefano Casiraghi, he was killed in a speedboat crash in 1990. Stéphanie has so far been divorced twice and had three children born out of wedlock. And Albert, notoriously commitment-phobic, had two illegitimate children with different mothers before marrying Charlene Wittstock, a former South African Olympic swimmer, in 2011.

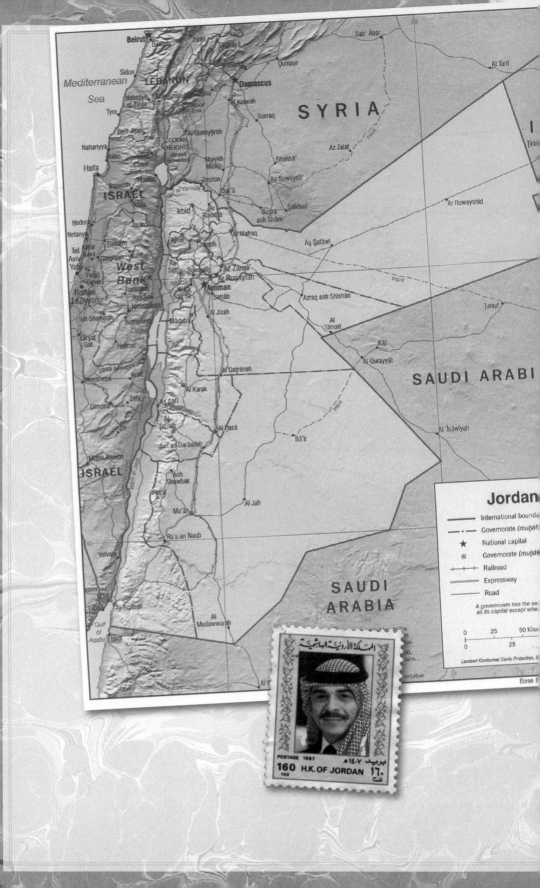

King Hussein of Jordan
– & –
Lisa Halaby

Hussein bin Talal
Born: November 14, 1935, Amman, Jordan Died: February 7, 1999, Amman, Jordan

Lisa Najeeb Halaby
Born: August 23, 1951, Washington, D.C.

Married: June 15, 1978

King Hussein of Jordan & Lisa Halaby

He enjoyed an exciting, extravagant lifestyle: flying planes, parachute jumping, racing motorcycles

American career girl Lisa Halaby had to think long and hard when King Hussein proposed. He was sixteen years older than her, had eight children from three previous marriages, and was head of an Arab state that was in the front line of Middle East conflict. Was she ready to be a Queen? Did she even want to be?

*A*t the age of sixteen Hussein bin Talal was attending Friday prayers with his much-loved grandfather at the Al-Aqsa mosque in Jerusalem when a gunman appeared from nowhere, shot and killed his grandfather, and fired at him. Hussein's life was only saved by a medal he was wearing on his military uniform, which deflected the bullet. It was a shocking introduction to what could be expected for a monarch who attempted to broker peace between Israel and its Arab neighbors, but it didn't deter Hussein from following exactly the same path.

He had just finished his studies at Harrow School in England when he became King of Jordan, and he went on to do a course at Sandhurst Military Academy before assuming full royal duties. From the start, his twin goals were to achieve peace in the Middle East and to improve the lives of his country's people, and he worked hard to achieve both ends—yet he still had time to gain something of a playboy reputation along the way. He was a handsome man who loved dancing and parties, and women flocked to him. He enjoyed an exciting lifestyle: flying planes, parachute jumping, racing motorcycles, or trying out high-performance cars in the Jordanian desert. Media stories of his female conquests began to appear in the press and would taint his reputation in the decades to come.

A king needs a wife, and in 1955 he married his Egyptian-born third cousin Sharifa Dina bint 'Abdu'l-Hamid. They had a daughter, but the marriage was a failure and they separated in 1956. In 1961 he married a British woman, Antoinette Gardiner, with whom he had four children, but they divorced a decade later. Then in 1972 he married Alia, daughter of a

OPPOSITE
Hussein was a skilled helicopter pilot.

BELOW
Hussein with his first wife Sharifa in 1955. They met while studying in London, but found after marriage they had little in common. She went on to marry a high-ranking official in the Palestinian Liberation Organization (PLO).

ASSASSINATION ATTEMPTS

After the assassination of his grandfather, Hussein always kept a gun close at hand—with good reason, as there would be at least twelve attempts on his life during his reign (some say many more). In the late 1950s, Syrian MiG fighters attacked a plane in which he was flying with his uncle and almost brought it down. His Egyptian valet once filled a bottle of nose drops with acid, a plot that was discovered when the bottle fell in a sink and broke and the contents began to eat through the ceramic. In a separate incident a palace cook was bribed by Syrian intelligence to attempt to poison him. There were at least two ambushes, one on the road from the airport when his uncle managed to push the King out of the car, and another when his convoy was fired upon as he drove to his farm. The Jordanians said Hussein possessed *baraka*, or God's blessing, for surviving all these attempted murders.

RIGHT
King Hussein, 1970. In his memoirs he wrote that the first thing he learned as monarch was "the unimportance of death: that when you have to die, you die."

Jordanian diplomat, and three more children were born. She was popular as queen but died tragically in a helicopter crash in 1977. Hussein now had plenty of heirs but no one with whom to share the pressures and responsibilities of royal life, no one with whom he could relax and talk in complete confidence at the end of the day.

King Hussein had already met Lisa Halaby before Queen Alia died. Her father was an international advisor to Jordan's national airline and Lisa accompanied him to a celebration in the winter of 1976 to mark the acquisition of the fleet's first Boeing 747. She met King Hussein, Queen Alia, and the couple's eldest daughter on the tarmac of Amman airport that day, but she could have had no inkling that within two years she would be the girl's stepmother—and Hussein's fourth wife.

A HIGH-FLIER

Lisa Halaby came from an unusual mixture of backgrounds. Her father's family were Syrian Christians who had emigrated to the United States in 1891, while her mother was a tall, blonde beauty of Swedish descent. The Arab ancestors were hard-working entrepreneurs who set up their own successful import-export business and her father had been a test pilot during World War II, flying more than fifty different kinds of planes. After the war, he worked as an aircraft advisor in Saudi Arabia, then became head of the US Federal Aviation Authority, followed by CEO of PanAm Airways. His career meant that the family had to move around a lot during Lisa's childhood, which she credited with giving her a sense of independence and self-sufficiency. She was educated at prestigious schools—the National Cathedral School in Washington, D.C., the Chapin School in New York, Concord Academy in Massachusetts—before studying architecture and urban planning at Princeton.

After graduation, Lisa worked for a year in Australia with a company that planned new towns, then with a British architectural firm in Tehran—an experience that brought her into contact with Arab culture and encouraged her to explore her own Arabic roots. After that she took a temporary job with her father's aviation company in Jordan, and was working there when she heard the shocking news of Queen Alia's death in a helicopter crash. She had been planning to go back to America to take a journalism course at Columbia University when, in mid-1977, she was offered a job designing the Jordanian airline's facilities worldwide. It was too good an opportunity to pass up.

In her new job, Lisa occasionally came into contact with King Hussein and he always teased her, seeming to enjoy making her blush. She was tall, blonde, beautiful, and a smart career woman, and he found himself irresistibly drawn to her. On April 7, 1978, he asked her to lunch to advise him on some building problems in his palace complex—a lunch date that lasted until 7:30 that evening, and at which he introduced her to his three youngest children and gave her a tour of the royal stables. She was flattered by his attention but didn't

She was tall, blonde, beautiful, and a smart career woman, and he found himself irresistibly drawn to her

ABOVE
While Lisa was working in Tehran in 1976, an acquaintance read her fortune from the grounds in her coffee cup: "You will marry someone high-born," he said, "an aristocrat from the land of your ancestors."

ABOVE
Queen Noor with King Hussein in 1989, by which time they had been married eleven years and had four children. She also helped to raise his three children by Queen Alia but had a more distant relationship with the offspring of his first two marriages.

think anything of it, since she was only twenty-six years old to his forty-two. He told her later that he had already fallen in love with her at this stage.

A week after the lunch date, Lisa was invited to the King's holiday home in Aqaba for the weekend, where she met the rest of his children. The couple began dining together every night and going for long motorcycle rides through the desert or flights in his personal helicopter. Aware of Hussein's playboy reputation, her father warned her to be careful, but events were moving faster than he could have anticipated. On April 25, just over two weeks after their first date, Hussein stunned Lisa by asking if he might call her father to request her hand in marriage. Completely taken by surprise, she asked for time to think it over. She had several questions to consider. Would the Jordanian people and, indeed, the Arab world, accept a queen born in the United States at a time when there was so much anti-American sentiment in the region? Would Hussein's eight children accept her? Did she have the self-discipline for all that was required of those in a royal position? And what about her own career? She was too independent to be a stay-at-home wife. Besides, Hussein was Muslim and she had been raised a Christian.

For two weeks, Lisa mulled over her decision, while the couple continued to dine together every evening. She watched the warmth with which King Hussein dealt with those around him, and realized he was a man "full of character, decency and conviction." And, as she admitted later in her autobiography, "I was also deeply attracted to him." On May 13, Hussein asked again, "Shall I call your father?" And Lisa replied simply, "Yes."

ADJUSTING TO ROYAL LIFE

Before they married, Lisa made the decision to become a Muslim. Her husband-to-be hadn't insisted upon it, but the more she learned about the religion, the more she felt an affinity with it.

She relinquished her American citizenship and became a Jordanian. She also had to get used to the new Arabic name her fiancé gave her: Noor Al-Hussein, which means Light of Hussein. The three youngest children, those he'd had with Alia, were delighted to be gaining a stepmother and although she hardly knew the others, Lisa hoped to win them over in time. The wedding at Zahran Palace was simple and, as is traditional, Lisa was the only woman present. The ceremony involved the signing of a contract and the repetition of vows. It all took no more than five minutes, but the room was full of international photographers and the next day her picture was on the front page of newspapers around the world. The couple honeymooned in Scotland and then London before flying back to Amman to start married life, with Lisa now to be known as Queen Noor.

She soon realized the difficulties of having any private time with her husband, who was constantly in demand and surrounded by aides. There were people everywhere and, as she later recalled, "the bathroom . . . was the only place where we could talk with complete freedom." She found it difficult being addressed by the impersonal "Your Majesty" instead of simply "Lisa," and before long she had become a target for the anti-American press in Jordan. Rumors spread that the CIA had arranged the helicopter crash in which the previous queen died in order to get an American on the throne, and there were almost daily stories of the new queen's "vast extravagance" and of early problems in the marriage caused by his philandering. In fact, Lisa had very simple tastes, preferring jeans and no makeup to ball gowns and tiaras, but that wouldn't stop the rumor

BELOW
Hussein and Noor with Princess Iman, born in April 1983. During the First Gulf War of 1990– 91, their children stayed in Austria with her sister.

THE KING & QUEEN'S LEGACY

King Hussein and Queen Noor
greatly improved the lives of
ordinary Jordanians with their
infrastructure projects and health
and education initiatives. In 1950,
only 10 percent of homes had
water, electricity, and sanitation,
but by the end of his reign 99
percent did. Literacy climbed
from 33 percent in 1960 to
85.5 percent in 1996. And child
mortality fell dramatically from
seventy deaths per thousand
births in 1981 to thirty-seven
per thousand in 1991, according
to UNICEF figures. Noor
campaigned on women's issues,
allying herself with causes such
as opposition to honor killings
and support for women in the
workplace. The people of Jordan
have more political freedom
than most in the region, and are
able to live generally peaceful
lives due to King Hussein's
covert diplomacy with his more
powerful neighbors. After the
King's death, Noor set up a
foundation in his memory,
the King Hussein Foundation
International, to promote peace
in the Middle East.

THIS PAGE
*Queen Noor and King Hussein worked
tirelessly to protect Jordan's extraordinary
ancient heritage, including the spectacular
rose-red city of Petra.*

mill. And, on the whole, she and King Hussein were very happy together, although his playboy past meant that every time he was photographed with another woman, for whatever reason, she was assumed to be a mistress.

King Hussein had far more pressing problems on his hands than worrying about the press. Throughout his reign he had been holding hours and hours of secret talks with Israeli leaders in an attempt to find a solution to the strife between their two countries and in the region at large. Even after the 1967 Arab–Israeli war, when Jordan lost control of Jerusalem and the West Bank, he kept channels of communication open and cultivated friendships with American as well as Middle Eastern rulers. Hussein saw himself in a position to be an honest broker between parties, and knew that his small country, lacking oil wealth, needed as many friends as it could get. However, he lost favor in the West in 1991 when he spoke out against the Gulf War and found himself sidelined in talks between Israel and the Palestinian Liberation Organization, who signed a peace agreement in 1993. Still, in July 1994, largely as a result of Hussein's efforts, Israel and Jordan, two neighbors with a long shared border, signed their own peace agreement, ending fifty years of war between them.

BELOW
The King and Queen with three of their children in 1995. She was often criticized by Jordanian citizens for getting involved in politics, for her Western style of dress, and for her views on women's rights. When she married Hussein there was no precedent for Jordanian spouses expressing their views in public.

"With you by my side, I celebrate each day"

"This is without doubt my proudest accomplishment: leaving my people a legacy of peace," King Hussein said shortly before the ceremony.

Queen Noor traveled with her husband on all his overseas trips and often spoke at conferences about Middle Eastern politics, but was frustrated to find that newspapers sent their fashion editors to report on what she was wearing rather than the substance of her speeches. She worked tirelessly for several organizations that were trying to improve life for the citizens of Jordan: the Noor Al Hussein Foundation was a blanket group dealing with poverty, health, education, and the rights of women and children; Seeds of Peace brought together children from around the Middle East; and United World Colleges, of which she became president in 1995, offered an education that brought together students from around the world. She stayed busy and used her intellect with these initiatives. On top of that, during the first six years of her marriage, she gave birth to two sons and two daughters. On their tenth wedding anniversary, Hussein left a note on her pillow thanking her for all she had done for him: "With you by my side, I celebrate each day," he wrote.

THE FINAL STRUGGLE

In 1992, King Hussein had a brush with cancer, which led to a kidney being removed. He recovered, but in 1998 he once more became ill, this time with non-Hodgkin's lymphoma, which was treated at the Mayo Clinic in Minnesota. He underwent six grueling courses of chemotherapy followed by a bone marrow transplant. Queen Noor was by his side throughout. In the midst of his treatment, in October 1998, Hussein rose from his bed, bald from the chemotherapy and very frail, to help President Bill Clinton conclude a new accord between Israeli and Palestinian negotiators: "We have no right to dictate through irresponsible action or narrow-mindedness the future of our children or their children's children," he said. It was a key intervention that led to the signing of the Wye River memorandum regarding Israeli withdrawal from the West Bank and Gaza Strip. Hussein's years of efforts for peace earned him a Nobel Peace Prize nomination that year.

He flew home to Jordan, seemingly in remission from the cancer, and took the unusual step of changing his line of succession. His brother Hassan had been Crown Prince for many years and expected to succeed; family friends say that Queen Noor wanted her eldest son Hamzah to have the throne; but instead, the king appointed his eldest son Abdullah. He wrote to Hassan explaining that he felt it was important to engage the next generation, and Hassan had no choice but to accept. Shortly afterward, it became apparent that the cancer had recurred. The family were gathered around his bedside in the palace in Amman as King Hussein died after forty-six years on the throne. "The king has died; long live the king," Queen Noor said, turning to hug Abdullah.

The funeral brought leaders from around the world to Jordan, so it was some time before Queen Noor was able to grieve quietly. She was comforted by a letter the king had written while at the Mayo Clinic, which spoke of her in glowing terms: "She, the Jordanian, who belongs to this country with every fiber of her being, holds her head high in the defense and service of this country's interest. . . . We have grown together in soul and mind." For herself, she wrote in her autobiography, "I continue to thank God for the leap of faith I made as a young woman. . . . I will try to bring my husband's spirit of optimism and moral conviction to everything I do. He never gave up, nor shall I."

BELOW
A historic moment on October 23, 1998. The bald King Hussein is applauded by, from left to right, Yasser Arafat of the PLO, US President Bill Clinton, and Israeli Prime Minister Benjamin Netanyahu, after rising from his sick bed to speak in support of peace at the Wye River summit.

Prince William
– & –
Catherine Middleton

William Arthur Philip Louis
Born: June 21, 1982, London, England

Catherine "Kate" Elizabeth Middleton
Born: January 9, 1982, Reading, England

Married: April 29, 2011

ABOVE
The royal wedding on April 29, 2011. Celebrity guests included David and Victoria Beckham, Sir Elton John and David Furnish, and Rowan Atkinson. Foreign royalty included the Queen of Spain, the Sultan of Brunei, the King and Queen of Norway, and the Emir of Qatar.

After witnessing his parents' marriage disintegrating in a vitriolic and very public way, then his mother's hounding by the media contributing to her death in a car crash, it's entirely understandable that William was wary of commitment. It would take a very patient and resilient girl to win his heart . . .

The poignant image of two young boys walking behind their mother's coffin, flanked by their father, grandfather, and uncle, seared itself on the consciousness of the two billion people who watched Princess Diana's funeral on television or on the Internet around the world. William was just fifteen years old and didn't want to do it, afraid he might break down, but he was finally persuaded by Prince Philip; it became the most unbearably sad sight of a somber day. William has known from early childhood that he was born into a life of obedience, duty, and responsibility. He is the eldest son of Queen Elizabeth II's eldest son and although his mother, Princess Diana, tried to give her boys an insight into what it meant to be poor and disadvantaged through her work with numerous charities, they would never be ordinary citizens. What ordinary boy has his own full-time bodyguard from Scotland Yard's Royalty and Diplomatic Protection Squad from birth?

Diana was a hands-on mother who didn't believe in banishing the children to the nursery, and who insisted on taking William on a royal tour of Australia and New Zealand when he was just nine months old because she couldn't bear to be parted from him. However, as he grew up she confided in him about the misery of her marriage, making William feel protective of her. By the time he went to Ludgrove boarding school at the age of eight, his parents were leading separate lives, although still married, and every rumor about them was front-page news, whether substantiated or not.

BELOW
Prince William, Charles Spencer, Prince Harry, and Prince Charles follow Diana's coffin on September 6, 1997. "There's not a day goes by when I don't think about it once," William said in 2007 at a Diana memorial concert.

ABOVE
Diana and William on
vacation in Majorca in
1987, as guests of King
Juan Carlos and Queen
Sofia. Diana was a hands-
on, fun mom despite her
personal troubles.

In 1995, he was attending Eton College in Windsor when his mother gave a television interview confessing to an affair with James Hewitt, the man who had taught her sons to ride, and famously commenting on Prince Charles's affair with his old flame Camilla Parker-Bowles: "There were three of us in this marriage, so it was a bit crowded." Many of William's school friends watched the broadcast, and for weeks afterward paparazzi prowled the nearby town of Windsor, trying to get shots of the schoolboy prince. William is said to have been mortified by the very public airing of his private life and by the media attention that followed, but he still adored his mother and when the divorce went through and Diana was stripped of her title of "Royal Highness," according to friends he promised he would restore it as soon as he became king.

William and his brother Harry were on vacation at the Queen's estate of Balmoral in Scotland when the news broke of their mother's death in a car crash in Paris while being pursued by paparazzi. She had spoken to William on the telephone the day before and he had expected to see her later that day. It was a devastating blow for a fifteen-year-old boy and it made him retreat into his shell, vowing never to trust the media, whom he blamed for his loss. It also made him very cautious about the friends he chose. "People who try to take advantage of me, and get a piece of me, I spot it quickly and soon go off them. I'm not stupid," he said in an interview before starting his studies at St. Andrew's University. That also made it difficult for girls who were interested in him. He was slow to make up his mind about potential girlfriends and he wanted to be the one who made the first move. Many simply didn't have the patience to wait.

UNIVERSITY LIFE

In September 2001, William arrived to study History of Art at St. Andrew's, an ancient and prestigious university in a tiny Scottish seaside town. He moved into St. Salvator's residence hall for his first year, along with a group of friends from Eton and the obligatory protection officers, and it wasn't long before he spotted a very pretty girl named Kate Middleton who was boarding in the same hall. William had met her once or twice before through mutual friends and they soon began chatting. Kate was studying the same art history course and agreed to share her notes with him when he was unable to attend a lecture. There was no romance at first, however. She began dating a fourth-year law student called Rupert Finch while William started seeing an English language and creative writing student called Carly Massy-Birch.

"People who try to take advantage of me, and get a piece of me, I spot it quickly and soon go off them. I'm not stupid"

As their friendship developed, William found that, like him, Kate was interested in sports; she had been in the netball, tennis, and hockey teams at school, and was a swimming champion. In fact, she had first caught sight of the young prince when he came with the Ludgrove team to play hockey at her prep school, St. Andrew's, when both were nine years old. They had also both been on gap years before starting university and, coincidentally, both had done volunteer work with the same organization in Chile.

CONSPIRACY THEORIES

Shortly after Princess Diana's death in a car crash in the Pont de l'Alma tunnel in Paris on August 31, 1997, Mohamed Al-Fayed, whose son Dodi had also died in the crash, claimed it had been arranged by Britain's secret services. He said that Diana and Dodi had been planning to marry and the royals could not stomach having a Muslim in the family. Conspiracy theorists leapt on reports that a white Fiat Uno had bumped into the Mercedes in which she was being driven shortly before it crashed into the tunnel wall; that a white strobe light had been used to blind the driver, Henri Paul; that Paul worked for French security services; that the tests on blood taken from him after the accident were contaminated; that the car's seatbelt had been tampered with; and that Diana had been pregnant. However, a French investigation in 1999 and a British inquest in 2007/08 both found that the accident was caused by Henri Paul having alcohol levels in his blood that were three times the French legal limit and losing control of the car while being chased by paparazzi.

They may have had several interests in common, but their backgrounds couldn't have been more different. She was the eldest daughter of Berkshire couple, Carole and Paul Middleton. Her father was a flight dispatcher at Heathrow Airport and her mother had been a flight attendant when they met. After her children were born, Carole started her own mail-order company, Party Pieces, supplying party accessories. On her mother's side, Kate's family was working class, her ancestors including Durham coal miners, sheep thieves who had been transported to Australia, a road sweeper, and a cleaningwoman. Her father's family was middle class and it was thanks to a trust fund set up by his ancestors that they were able to pay for Kate, her sister Pippa, and her brother James to attend private schools. Kate thrived at her prep school but was bullied so badly at Downe House boarding school, where she was less sophisticated than the worldly London pupils, that her parents removed her quickly. She did better at Marlborough school in Wiltshire, but was taller than her peers and wore braces on her teeth, making her shy with the opposite sex. Toward the end of her school career she blossomed, so that when she arrived at St. Andrew's fellow students voted her the prettiest girl in their hall of residence.

BELOW
The black and turquoise see-through knitted dress in which Kate caught the Prince's attention. Designed by fashion graduate Charlotte Todd, it later sold at auction for $130,900.

By Christmas 2001, William's relationship with Carly was on the rocks, and in March 2002, he suddenly saw Kate in a new light after she took part in a charity fashion show wearing a transparent dress over black underwear. "Wow, Kate's hot!" he remarked to a friend, and his flirtation with Kate at the party afterward made it clear his feelings for her had changed from friendship to something stronger. She was still involved with Rupert Finch, but he was a couple of years older and would be leaving St. Andrew's that summer. Over the next few months, as one romance faded out, another began. Kate agreed to move into a flat with William and two other friends for their second year, but they kept their relationship completely under wraps, never arriving or leaving events together, so that only their very closest friends knew they were a couple.

It was June 2003 before the media first began to suspect Kate could be a royal girlfriend when William attended her twenty-first birthday party, but they were thrown off the trail at his own twenty-first when he sat at the head table with Jecca Craig, a close friend from Kenya. In an interview at this time, William claimed to be single, saying, "There's been a lot of speculation about every single girl I am with, and it does irritate me after a while, the more so because it is a complete pain for the girls." For their third year of university, William and Kate lived together with another housemate, Oli Baker, in a country cottage outside St. Andrew's where they enjoyed peace and privacy. They often had close friends over for dinner, but avoided the town's hotspots, so the media were left guessing the true situation. Like so many university romances, though, theirs foundered after graduation. William wanted his freedom over the summer and they agreed to take a break from the relationship. It must have been agonizing for Kate to read in the press about his vacations and to hear through the grapevine that he was pursuing an heiress called Isabella Anstruther-Gough-Calthorpe, but she sat tight and by October they were back together again.

When asked in April 2005 about his and Kate's prospects, William replied, "I'm only twenty-two, for God's sake. I'm too young to marry at my age. I don't want to get married till I'm at least twenty-eight or thirty." For Kate, who had already decided he was the love of her life, this must have been a blow. It was going to take all the patience and strength she could muster to hang on for another six years.

BELOW
The Queen inspects her grandson at the Sovereign's Parade, Sandhurst, December 2006. William graduated with the rank of second lieutenant.

THE WAITING GAME

While William pursued his career, doing military training at Sandhurst then qualifying as a search-and-rescue Royal Air Force helicopter pilot, there were long periods when Kate didn't see him. Meanwhile, she took a job as an accessories buyer for women's fashion store Jigsaw, followed by experience working as a photographer for her parents' company. Over Christmas 2006, the couple reached another crisis point after William was photographed talking to other girls in nightclubs. Kate was prepared to wait for him, but she didn't want to be humiliated and she gave him an ultimatum: commit or break up. By Easter 2007, they had agreed to separate. She was distraught but wore a brave face in public. Her dresses got shorter, her necklines lower, and she was frequently photographed going to nightclubs with her sister Pippa. "Look what you're missing," was the message to William. She also volunteered to take part in a charity dragon boat race in support of children's hospices, which involved training sessions

BELOW
Kate and William at the official announcement of their engagement on November 16, 2010. Diana's sapphire and diamond ring glitters on her finger.

at the crack of dawn with a team of women known as the Sisterhood. "Kate was very down and I think training became her therapy," said one of her teammates, Emma Sayle.

In fact, Kate and William never lost touch, and by that summer they had decided to give the relationship another chance. In August 2007, they vacationed on a remote island in the Seychelles and made a pact. William explained that he was still not ready to get married, but promised he would not let her down if she was willing to hang on until the time felt right. She agreed to wait. It must have been very frustrating, particularly when the British media began to refer to her as "Waity Katie," but it gave her time to learn how to cope with the pressures of royal life. Prince Charles's press officers were on hand to offer advice, but she admitted to a friend that she found the full-on attention "a little creepy." She had panic buttons installed in her home and tried to keep a low profile, but at the same time showed she was prepared to sue for breach of privacy after she was photographed playing tennis on a private court at Christmas 2009. Speculation about an engagement continued and Kate and William kept a chart on the bedroom wall at Clarence

He asked Kate to be his wife, presenting her with his mother's diamond and sapphire engagement ring

ABOVE
When William and Kate attended a gala dinner six weeks after their wedding, the tabloid press were disappointed there was no "baby bump" visible under the slinky evening gown.

House, his father's home, on which they added a tick for each news story claiming they were about to marry. There was a huge tick after he landed his Royal Air Force helicopter in a field behind Kate's family home in April 2008 and another after she was formally introduced to the Queen at a wedding the following month.

Then, in October 2010, William invited Kate on vacation to Kenya and took her to Lake Alice, one of the most remote spots in the world, where they stayed in a log cabin and fished in the lake. It was there, on October 20, that he went down on bended knee and asked Kate to be his wife, presenting her with his mother's diamond and sapphire engagement ring, which he had been carefully hiding in his backpack. "It was very romantic. I really didn't expect it . . .

PRINCES & COMMONERS

Before the 16th century, many English princes married commoners, but in 1660 there was strong disapproval from Samuel Pepys when James II married Anne Hyde, a lawyer's daughter, after getting her pregnant. "The . . . marriage hath undone the kingdom," he wrote indignantly. Thereafter, it was felt that royals should marry other royals and by Queen Victoria's day any royal personage who chose a spouse of lesser rank risked banishment and loss of military status. Such marriages were deemed "morganatic," meaning their children were not royal and royal inheritances did not pass down the line. Princess Mary of Teck, who married George V, was the product of a morganatic marriage and was not allowed to use the title "Royal Highness" as a result. In the 20th century, when royalty had begun to wane, many European royal families turned to the aristocracy to choose their spouses. Lady Diana Spencer, Prince William's mother, came from one of Britain's oldest and best-known aristocratic families, as did Elizabeth Bowes-Lyon, the Queen Mother. By the time William proposed to Kate, the taboo had been completely broken since in 2005 his father had married Camilla Parker-Bowles—a commoner and a divorcee as well, thus breaking yet another taboo.

It was a total shock . . . and very exciting," Kate said at the press photo call after their engagement was announced several weeks later. William explained why he had given her Diana's ring—"It was my way of making sure my mother didn't miss out on today"—but was careful to say, "No one is trying to fill my mother's shoes."

Why the long delay? They had known each other for over ten years and had been dating for over eight before tying the knot. William explained, smiling affectionately at Kate: "I wanted to give her a chance to see in and back out if she needed to." He was anxious that no other woman should be subjected to what his mother went through without the full support of the palace to help her deal with it. And no doubt he needed to make sure that Kate was tough enough for the job—which she has proved to be in spades.

They married on April 29, 2011, in Westminster Abbey, where Diana's funeral had taken place fourteen years earlier. There were 1,900 guests, including family friends, foreign heads of state, and members of the royal household. Kate looked stunning in a satin and lace dress made by Sarah Burton of design house Alexander McQueen, and the ceremony, which proceeded without so much as a hiccup, was watched in 180 countries around the world. In July 2013, Kate gave birth to an heir to the throne, whom they named George, a little boy who would have been Diana's first grandchild. The media follow Kate as they followed Diana, making personal comments on her post-pregnancy figure and scrutinizing every fashion choice, but she seems to deal with the attention with courtesy and an unruffled sense of humor. She is only the second commoner to marry into the British royal family in 350 years, and it may be that a touch of the steely determination of those working-class ancestors was exactly what was needed to win the hand of a prince whose early years were so traumatic.

OPPOSITE
William and Kate always look very natural together, far removed from the awkwardness that existed between his mother and father, who had to be prompted by photographers to display affection even in the early days of their marriage.

BELOW
Prince George was born on July 22, 2013, at St. Mary's Hospital in London, and immediately became third in line to the British throne after his father and grandfather.

Peter I of Portugal & Inês de Castro

Rodrigues, Dulce. "The Dead Queen or The Love Story of Pedro and Ines." NATO bulletin, February 1998.

Wheeler, Douglas L. and Opello, Walter C., Jr. *Historical Dictionary of Portugal.* New York, Scarecrow Press: 2010.

Shah Jahan & Mumtaz Mahal

Koch, Ebba. *The Complete Taj Mahal and the Riverfront Gardens of Agra.* London, Thames & Hudson: 2006

Preston, Diana. *A Teardrop on the Cheek of Time: The Story of the Taj Mahal.* New York, Transworld: 2007.

Catherine the Great & Grigory Potemkin

Cruse, Markus and Hoogenboom, Hilde (trans.). *The Memoirs of Catherine the Great.* New York, Modern Library Classics: 2005.

Montefiore, Simon Sebag. *Catherine the Great & Potemkin.* London, Vintage: 2000.

Smith, Douglas. *Love and Conquest: Personal Correspondence of Catherine the Great and Prince Grigory Potemkin.* DeKalb, IL, Northern Illinois University Press: 2004

Louis XVI & Marie Antoinette

Fraser, Antonia. *Marie Antoinette.* New York, Anchor: 2001.

Hibbert, Christopher. *The Days of the French Revolution.* London, Penguin: 2002.

Schama, Simon. *Citizens: A Chronicle of the French Revolution.* New York, Penguin: 1989.

Napoleon Bonaparte & Joséphine de Beauharnais

Aronson, Theo. *Napoleon and Josephine: A Love Story.* London, John Murray: 1990.

McLynn, Frank. *Napoleon.* London, Pimlico: 1998.

Thompson, J.M. (ed.) *Napoleon's Letters.* London, J.M. Dent & Sons: 1954.

Ludwig I of Bavaria & Lola Montez

Morton, James. *Lola Montez: Her Life & Conquests.* London, Portrait: 2007.

Seymour, Bruce. *Lola Montez, a Life.* London, Yale University Press: 1996.

Victor Emmanuel II & Rosa Vercellana

Abele, Truffa. *La Bella Rosin, Regina Senza Corona.* Moncalvo, Edizione Il Cenacolo: 1969

Godkin, G.S. *Life of Victor Emmanuel II.* London, Macmillan: 1880

Mack Smith, Denis. *Vittorio Emmanuele II.* Milan, Mondadori: 1995.

Rudolph, Crown Prince of Austria & Baroness Mary Vetsera

Barkeley, Richard. *The Road to Mayerling.* New York, St Martin's Press: 1958.

Franzel, Emil. *Crown Prince Rudolph and the Mayerling Tragedy: Fact and Fiction.* Vienna, Verlag Herold: 1974.

Nicholas II & Alexandra

Fuhrmann, Joseph T. (ed. and trans.). *The Complete Wartime Correspondence of Czar Nicholas II and the Empress Alexandra.* Westport, CT, Greenwood: 1999.

Massie, Robert K. *Nicholas and Alexandra*. London, Little Brown: 1967.

Massie, Robert K. *The Romanovs, The Final Chapter*. London, Jonathan Cape: 1995.

Edward VIII & Wallis Simpson

Bloch, Michael. *The Secret File of the Duke of Windsor*. London, Bantam: 1988

Higham, Charles. *Wallis: Secret Lives of the Duchess of Windsor*. London, Sidgwick & Jackson: 1988.

Sebba, Anne. *That Woman: the Life of Wallis Simpson, Duchess of Windsor*. London, Weidenfeld & Nicolson: 2011.

Ziegler, Philip. *King Edward VIII: the Official Biography*. New York, Alfred A. Knopf: 1991.

Prince Bertil of Sweden & Lilian Craig

The Economist obituary of Lilian Craig, March 16, 2013.

New York Times obituary of Lilian Craig, March 11, 2013.

Petersens, Fabian af. *Prins Bertil, ett liv*. Stockholm, T. Fischer: 1992.

Prince Rainier III & Grace Kelly

Spada, James. *Grace: Secret Lives of a Princess*. New York, Doubleday: 1987.

Spoto, Donald. *High Society, The Life of Grace Kelly*. New York, Three Rivers Press: 2009.

Telegraph obituary of Prince Rainier III of Monaco, April 7, 2005.

The Times obituary of Prince Rainier III of Monaco, April 6, 2005.

King Hussein of Jordan & Lisa Halaby

HM King Hussein of Jordan. *Uneasy Lies the Head*. New York, William Morrow & Co: 1962.

New York Times obituary of King Hussein, February 8, 1999.

Queen Noor. *Leap of Faith, Memoirs of an Unexpected Life*. London, Weidenfeld & Nicolson: 2003.

Prince William & Catherine Middleton

Moody, Marcia. *Kate: The Biography*. London, Michael O'Mara: 2013.

Nicholl, Katie. *The Making of a Royal Romance*. London, Arrow: 2011.

Smith, Sean. *Kate*. London, Simon & Schuster: 2012.

Akg-images/Album/Oronoz: 25

Bridgeman Art Library/Odessa Fine Arts Museum, Ukraine: 46; Private Collection/Dinodia: 34; Racconigi Castle, Piedmont, Italy/De Agostini Picture Library/A. Dagli Orti: 95

Corbis/Bettmann: 81R, 150

DBKing: 6B

Dreamstime.com/Georgios Kollidas: 83, 84

Holger Ellgaard: 148

Getty Images/AFP: 153; Apic: 75; The British Library: 39; Central Press: 15, 168; Jodi Cobb/National Geographic: 171; De Agostini: 6T, 8, 86; Fine Art Images/ Heritage Images: 121; Fratelli Alinari/ Alinari Archives, Florence: 99; Hulton Archive: 47, 63, 122B; Anwar Hussein: 187; Anwar Hussein/WireImage: 19; IBL Bildbyra/Heritage Images: 145; Imagno: 11, 114B, 115; Keystone: 133, 137; Keystone-France/Gamma-Keystone: 141, 151; Leemage/UIG: 93L; Mark Cuthbert/UK Press: 186; Michou Simon/Paris Match Archive: 159; Mondadori Porfolio: 160; MP/Leemage: 118; Joyce Naltchayan/AFP: 175; OFF/AFP/Getty Images: 2B, 139; Planet News Archive/SSPL: 146; Popperfoto: 139B; Prisma/UIG: 26; Carl de Souza/AFP: 178; STF/AFP: 165; Three Lions: 62; James Whitmore/Time Life Pictures: 167

ImageCollect.com/Featureflash: 177; Globe Photos: 17, 18, 129, 130L, 130R, 138, 140, 154L, 154R, 155, 156, 157, 158, 161B, 162, 166, 169, 170, 173, 176R, 179, 180, 182, 183; StarMaxWorldwide: 7, 184, 185

iStock/Duncan1890: 48, 73; Hulton-Archive: 9, 10, 13, 14, 20T, 29, 50L, 12, 82

Library of Congress, Washington, D.C.: 2T, 88, 20B, 32B, 42, 44B, 51, 52, 54, 56B, 57R, 57L, 59, 64, 65, 66, 67, 68B, 69L, 71, 72, 74, 78, 90, 100B, 105L, 107, 109B, 111, 116B, 117L, 117R, 124R, 124L, 126, 127B, 127T, 132, 140, 144L, 144R, 147, 152L, 164T

Los Angeles County Museum of Art: 32T, 35, 37, 40, 41

Mary Evans Picture Library: 22; Epic/ Tallandier: 21; Grenville Collins Postcard Collection: 33; Illustrated London News Ltd: 122T; John Frost Newspapers; 135T; Sueddeutsche Zeitung Photo: 76

NGA Images: 56T, 58, 61

© Österreichisches Staatsarchiv: 106B, 108

Press Association Images/Scanpix: 142

Scala, Florence: 27

Shutterstock: 152R, 161T; Antonio Abrignani: 100T, 102, 103; Solodov Alexey: 116T; Bocman1973: 162B; Paul Cowan: 28; Frank Fischbach: 89; Sigurcamp: 94; Silky: 30; Steven Wright: 176L; Stocksnapper: 97; Konstantin Yolshin: 172; TerraceStudio: 176T

Thinkstock: 60, 79, 85, 125, 134